Istanbul

Select

contents

Istanbul overview

If ever there was a happening city it has to be Istanbul, a great metropolis that has served as the capital of three great empires and is still today, while not the actual capital of Turkey – a privilege held by distant Ankara – the de facto capital when it comes to anything to do with art, culture, shopping and gastronomy.

Byzantium, Constantinople, Istanbul – whatever you choose to call it, the city simply reeks of exotic history. As soon as you set foot in Unesco-listed Old Istanbul, you will feel yourself being transported back in time to the days when Constantine the Great declared the city the capital of the Eastern Roman Empire before bequeathing Christianity to it on his deathbed; to the days when the Byzantine Emperor Justinian and his minx of a wife Theodora paid for the building of Hagia Sophia,

the stupendous church that provided a model for Mimar Sinan's later mosques; to the days when the power of the Ottoman sultans dominated the Eastern Mediterranean, a power still easy to imagine as you examine the wealth and luxury on display in the Topkapı Palace.

For independent travellers the good news is that Istanbul is still under-visited in comparison with hectic London, Paris and Rome. True, the crowds press heavily on the major sites of Sultanahmet, but there are still many hidden corners, such as the areas around the Süleymaniye and Fatih mosques. Explore remoter museums such as the Sakıp Sabancı or the Sadberk Hanım and you are unlikely to be disturbed by other visitors.

Not so long ago a place where the kebab ruled unchallenged in restaurants citywide, Istanbul is fast transforming into a centre for innovative gourmet dining. Ditto when it comes to cutting-edge shopping possibilities, especially in the backstreets of Beyoğlu.

in the mood for...

... Ottoman atmosphere

To get a feel for Ottomania you really have to start your explorations in the **Topkapı Palace** *(p.26)*, sizing up the kaftans of the sultans, gazing at the egg-sized emeralds and admiring the cool, tiled bedrooms of the Harem. But Ottoman style crops up all over town. You will find it in the graceful caiques used to ferry the sultans, on display at the **Naval Museum** *(p.122)*. You will find it in **Cağaloğlu Hamam** *(p.50)*, the grandest of the Turkish baths. And you will find it in restaurants, such as **Asitane** *(p.74)*, which specialise in serving the palace cuisine originally developed to tickle the taste buds of the sultans. Ottoman atmosphere lingers aromatically over the **Çorlulu Ali Paşa Medresesi** *(p.63)*, where locals come to smoke a *nargile* with the tourists. And it lingers too in the coffee grains when you try a real Turkish coffee in the grounds of the **Museum of Turkish and Islamic Arts** *(p.38)*. But most of all it lingers at the *semas* in Galata, where the **whirling dervishes** go

... romance

Just being in exotic Istanbul should be romance enough for most, but for a real Romeo and Juliet of an evening make a dinner reservation at one of the **Bosphorus fish restaurants** where the waiters are expert at making ther guests feel special (*p.169*). Or take the cable car up to the **Pierre Loti Café** (*p.141*) in Eyüp and savour a view that once captivated a true French romantic.

... family fun

Busy Istanbul has not traditionally offered much in the way of organised entertainment for children, although one place guaranteed to enthral is the hands-on **Rahmi M. Koç Museum** of industrial heritage (*p.145*). Boys will no doubt rave about the **1453 Panorama Museum** (*p.72*). And few youngsters will fail to enjoy a ferry ride up the **Bosphorus** (*p.156*) or along the **Golden Horn** (*p.138*). **Gülhane Park** (*p.40*) is a great place to let off a bit of steam, or why not feed the pigeons with the locals in front of the **New Mosque** (*p.89*)?

in the mood for...

... shop, shop, shopping

When it comes to shopping in Istanbul all roads lead to the **Grand Bazaar** *(p.52)*, a labyrinthine mash-up of shops selling everything from garish gold bracelets intended as wedding presents to luxurious fabrics just perfect for the maximalist bedroom. Keener on food shopping? Then home in on the **Spice Market** *(p.88)*, where you can pick up souvenir packets of tea with fellow tourists or elbow the locals outside for Turkish regional cheeses. Alternatively, give the **Balat** or **Kadıköy markets** *(p.146 and p.166)* a whirl. Historic **Turkish delight** *(p.93)* from Eminönü makes a great gift, as do any of the myriad sweets on offer at **Koska** *(p.59)*. For antiques, the place to go is **Çukurcuma** in Beyoğlu *(p.111)*, while in Sultanahmet there are **carpet shops** galore *(p.39)*. You can land yourself a new take on an old handicraft, such as a felt shawl, around **Küçük Aya Sofya** *(p.43)*, while at **Laleli Mosque** you can stock up on soap made from olive oil *(p.58)*. For classy souvenirs, head straight for the **Arasta Bazaar** *(p.31)*, or shop for the quirky and handmade at the **Ortaköy Craft Market** *(p.130)* on Sunday.

8

... street eats

Want to grab a bite on the go? Then head straight down to the Eminönü waterfront, where **fish sandwiches, pickles** *(p.92)* and filling *simits (p.87)* are yours for the asking. Up in Beyoğlu, the place to go is the **Balık Pazarı**, or Fish Market, where you can tuck into fried mussels or *kokoreç (p.108)*. Alternatively, nip up to **Ortaköy** for one of the biggest baked potatoes you have ever seen *(p.130)*, or across to **Süleymaniye** to tuck into baked beans with the locals *(p.60)*.

... learning a new skill

What do you mean, you're on holiday? That's no excuse to put your feet up! To learn how to wow your friends with a home-cooked Turkish meal book straight onto a course at **Alaturca** *(p.36)* and find out how it is done. To gen up on the wines to go with the food head for the **Kayra Academy** *(p.115)*, so you can go home a true Turkish oenophile. Finally, drop in on the *medrese* at Küçük Aya Sofya and learn how to **marble paper** *(p.43)* ready to send out superior invitations.

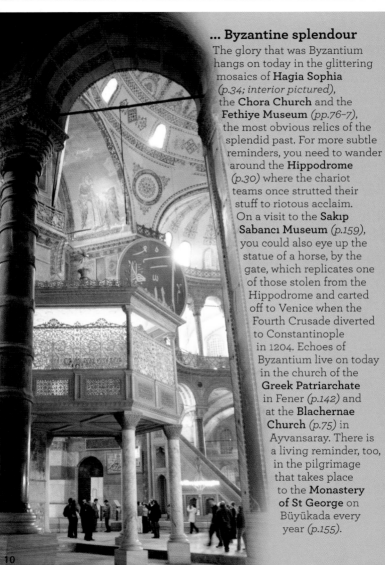

... Byzantine splendour

The glory that was Byzantium hangs on today in the glittering mosaics of **Hagia Sophia** (*p.34; interior pictured*), the **Chora Church** and the **Fethiye Museum** (*pp.76-7*), the most obvious relics of the splendid past. For more subtle reminders, you need to wander around the **Hippodrome** (*p.30*) where the chariot teams once strutted their stuff to riotous acclaim. On a visit to the **Sakıp Sabancı Museum** (*p.159*), you could also eye up the statue of a horse, by the gate, which replicates one of those stolen from the Hippodrome and carted off to Venice when the Fourth Crusade diverted to Constantinople in 1204. Echoes of Byzantium live on today in the church of the **Greek Patriarchate** in Fener (*p.142*) and at the **Blachernae Church** (*p.75*) in Ayvansaray. There is a living reminder, too, in the pilgrimage that takes place to the **Monastery of St George** on Büyükada every year (*p.155*).

... a night on the town

When it comes to lively nightlife you can generally forget about Sultanahmet. Over in Beyoğlu, however, when the sun goes down it's time to party at **Babylon**, **Roxy** or **Ghetto** *(p.116)*, or in the *meyhanes* of **Nevizade Sokak** *(p.112)*. After something a little more olde worlde? Then you could always prop up the bar in the famous **Pera Palas Hotel** *(p.105)*, redolent of the era of the Orient Express. To live it up with Istanbul's student crowd, head straight for Barlar Sokak in **Kadıköy** *(p.167)* or to the *nargile* cafés of **Tophane** *(p.91)*.

... a lazy day

If you are tiring of seeing the sights, you might want to head out to one of the Princes' Islands, such as **Büyükada** *(p.155)*, where you can hop into a phaeton *(pictured)* and clip-clop your way round the island in slow and laid-back style. Lounging about on one of the long **Bosphorus cruises** *(p.156)* or shorter **Golden Horn ferry rides** *(p.138)* is guaranteed to have you recharging the batteries in no time.

in the mood for...

... contemporary art

Modern Istanbul has a vibrant arts scene which really got into its stride with the opening of the **Istanbul Modern** (p.90; pictured) in 2005. Since then it has been joined by the even more cutting-edge scene that is **SantralIstanbul** (p.139), where art is displayed in a former power station. Smaller galleries with changing exhibitions dot **İstiklal Caddesi** (pp.107–8) in Beyoğlu. The **Pera Museum** (p.104) houses a fine collection of landscape paintings of Istanbul as well as Osman Hamdi Bey's famous painting of a tortoise trainer.

... offbeat exploration

Everybody wanders along **Divan Yolu** (p.32), and many make it over to bustling **İstiklal Caddesi** (p.109) too, but for a wonderful walk off the beaten track head to vibrant **Ortaköy** (p.130) with its stunning mosque (pictured), or to Bebek where you can stroll along the waterside promenade to **Rumeli Hisarı** (p.161) with only Turks for company. Hop off the ferry in **Arnavutköy** (p.160) and you are unlikely to have many companions; walk up Barbaros Bulvarı to the **Şeyh Zafir Mosque** (p.128) in Beşiktaş and you will almost certainly have it to yourself.

... dinner with a view

In a city renowned for its spectacular views, landing a table for dinner that lets you enjoy good food while also gazing out over the Bosphorus, Sea of Marmara or Golden Horn has to be the ultimate goal. In Beyoğlu, **Mikla**, **360** *(pictured)* and **Leb-i Derya** *(all p.113)* are the jewels in the crown when it comes to fine dining rolled up with watery vistas, while the **Zeyrekhane Restaurant** *(p.80)* treats its clientele to panoramic views of the Golden Horn. Cheaper, more casual views can be had from the **Galata Bridge** *(p.97)*. Eating fish so close to the water that you are almost sitting in it is an option at **İskele** in Rumeli Hisarı, and at **Poseidon** or **Bebek Balıkçısı** in Bebek *(all p.169)*. The Bosphorus views come with a healthy eating twist at **Abracadabra** in Arnavutköy *(p.160)* and with access to a gem of a museum at the **Muzedechanga** *(p.159)*. For wraparound views to go with your food, you could hardly do better than home in on the tiny **Maiden's Tower** in Üsküdar *(p.165)* or the decommissioned ferry terminal at **Moda** near Kadıköy *(p.167)*.

... history

Istanbul is above all else a city for history lovers. Whether your tastes run to the truly ancient, such as the **Çemberlitas Column** *(p.54)*, dating back to the reign of the Roman emperor Constantine the Great, or to the more recent such as the relics of the **Orient Express** train on display in Sirkeci Station *(p.94)*, there is something here for everyone. The **Museum of Archaeology** *(p.41)* brings it all up to date by showing off finds made in the city during excavation work for the Marmaray tunnel which is currently being drilled through the Bosphorus.

Most of the city's great historic monuments belong to either the Byzantine or Ottoman eras. For those who favour the Byzantines, must-see sights include the **remains of the Great Palace** in Sultanahmet *(p.29)*, the **Chora Church** *(p.76)* and of course **Hagia Sophia** *(p.34; pictured)*, the Emperor Justinian's great masterpiece without which Sinan's many domes might never have seen the light of day. A little less well known are **Küçük Aya Sofya** *(p.43)* and the **Kalenderhane Mosque** *(p.56)*, both Byzantine churches that

became mosques after the arrival of the Ottomans.

The Ottoman Conquest of the city in 1453 changed everything. To get an idea of what it might have been like to be alive on the day when the Ottomans burst through the Land Walls, head straight for the **1453 Panorama Museum** *(p.72)*, then press on into Fatih to inspect the **tomb of Mehmed the Conqueror** *(p.81)*, the 21-year-old Ottoman sultan who snatched Constantinople from the Byzantines. The city is studded with reminders of the prolific Ottoman architect Sinan, including his masterpiece, the **Süleymaniye Mosque** *(p.60)*, and the much less visited **Atik Valide and İskele mosques** in Üsküdar *(pp.162-3)*. **Topkapı Palace** *(p.26)* was home to the Ottoman sultans in their heyday, while the **Dolmabahçe and Yıldız palaces** *(p.126 and p.124)* served as retreats in the long years of imperial decline.

In 1923 Turkey became a republic and the capital was moved to Ankara. Mustafa Kemal Atatürk, the genius behind the many reforms that followed, died in the Dolmabahçe Palace in 1938.

... escaping the crowds

Istanbul may be relatively under-visited, but it is unlikely to feel that way on a summer afternoon when the cruise ships land their passengers on Topkapı Palace all at the same time. The good news is that there are plenty of places to escape the crowds – on **Burgaz or Kınalı islands** (p.154), for example, or while walking along the ancient **Land Walls** (pp.70–1). Museums such as the **Sakıp Sabancı** (p.159) and **Sadberk Hanım** (p.158) are rarely overrun with visitors, nor are the cute little **Küçüksu** or **Ihlamur pavilions** (pp.168 and 129). **Beylerbeyi Palace** (p.164) is much less busy than Dolmabahçe Palace, the **Fethiye Museum** less crowded than the Kariye Museum (p.77), and the **Sokullu Mehmed Paşa Mosque** (p.37) less visited than the Süleymaniye. Those who really want to give the crowds the slip can do so by taking themselves off to **Kadıköy** (pp.166–7) or **Üsküdar** (p.162; pictured) on the Asian shore. And you will find far fewer people exploring historic **Fener** (p.142) than Sultanahmet.

... being pampered

The Turks were into pampering long before the modern vogue for self-indulgence, with the hamams (Turkish baths) the greatest exponents of the Ottoman 'because you're worth it' philosophy. Today, you can still have a massage in the **Cağaloğlu Hamam**, the bath where Florence Nightingale soaped away the stresses of treating the injured from the Crimean battlefields; the **Süleymaniye Hamam** offers mixed bathing in an achingly historic building; **Çemberlitaş** separates the sexes more traditionally *(all p.50; Çemberlitaş pictured below)*. But with prices rising sharply, you might also want to seek out a more off-the-beaten-track bath experience, in which case the hamam attached to the **Mihrimah Sultan Mosque** *(p.73)* should do nicely.

More in the mood to go swimming? Then head for the **Çırağan Palace Kempinski Hotel** *(p.125)*, where a bathe in the infinity pool can be followed with English-style afternoon tea in the lap of absolute luxury.

neighbourhoods

The Bosphorus divides Istanbul into European and Asian sides, with the inlet of the Golden Horn further subdividing European Istanbul between Old Istanbul, the historic peninsula with most of the major sites, and Beyoğlu, the more modern quarter that rises uphill towards the Galata Tower. The Princes' Islands float serenely offshore in the Sea of Marmara.

Sultanahmet and Kumkapı Sultanahmet is the broad-brush name for the heart of Old Istanbul, the area around Hagia Sophia, the Blue Mosque (aka Sultanahmet Mosque) and the Topkapı Palace. With most of the big-ticket sites, it's where the majority of visitors spend their time, although it is still possible to escape the crowds by wandering a little away from Sultanahmet Square. Best known for its fish restaurants, Kumkapı remains a more authentic neighbourhood, though fast succumbing to tourism.

Beyazıt, Cağaloğlu and Süleymaniye Within walking distance of Sultanahmet, Beyazıt is best known for the exotic chaos of the sprawling Grand Bazaar, while Cağaloğlu is a great place in which to experience a massage in a historic hamam. Dominated by its mosque, the masterpiece of Ottoman architect Sinan, Süleymaniye is still a living part of the historic peninsula with many hidden corners.

Land Walls, Kariye and Fatih The Land Walls, originally financed by the Emperor Theodosius, mark the western edge of the historic peninsula and make a great walking trail for those who'd like to escape the crowds. Just inside the walls, Kariye is home to the Byzantine masterpiece of the Chora Church. A little further east the Fatih Mosque is the burial place of Sultan Mehmed the Conqueror.

Eminönü, Karaköy and Tophane Fringing the point where the Golden Horn meets the Sea of Marmara, Eminönü is a frantically busy wharf offering ferry connections to Üsküdar, Kadıköy and the Bosphorus. It is joined by the fishermen-festooned Galata Bridge to equally busy Karaköy. A tram stop east is Tophane, dominated by the old Ottoman arsenal building but better known today for its *nargile* (water-pipe) cafés.

Beyoğlu By far the liveliest part of the city, Beyoğlu is home to many of the glitziest hotels, restaurants and nightclubs, as well as to much of alternative Istanbul, a labyrinth of tiny art galleries and workshops that open and close with predictable unpredictability. Come here to marvel at the sheer quantity of people that can be squeezed into İstiklal Caddesi, the pedestrianised main thoroughfare.

Beşiktaş and Dolmabahçe In the 19th century the sultans abandoned Topkapı in favour of Dolmabahçe, just east of Tophane. Today, their 'new' palace is the first of a string of mansions stretching up to Beşiktaş, a busy residential suburb home to one of the city's favourite football teams.

The Golden Horn Separating Old Istanbul from Beyoğlu, the Golden Horn meanders up towards Eyüp, site of Istanbul's most revered mosque. On the way it bypasses the old Greek neighbourhood of Fener, the old Jewish suburb of Balat, and Hasköy where Turkey's first industrial museum stands on a site where Ottoman navy ships were once built.

The Rest of Istanbul For visitors, the most interesting parts of the outlying city are the many picturesque suburbs that line the Bosphorus, such as Ortaköy, Arnavutköy and Bebek, although Üsküdar and Kadıköy will appeal to those who want to get to grips with the modern city. In summer everyone heads for the Princes' Islands to escape the heat.

KURTULUŞ

MAÇKA PARKI

ŞİŞLİ

TAŞLIK PARKI

İnönü Stadyumu

TAKSİM PARKI

Taksim Meydanı (Taksim Square)

Atatürk Cultural Centre

Dolmabahçe Sarayı (Dolmabahçe Palace)

B E Y O Ğ L U

Hagia Triada

TAKSİM

Galatasaray Lisesi (Galatasaray Lycée)

TEPEBAŞI PARKI

Pera Müzesi (Pera Museum)

FINDIKLI PARKI

Galata Mevlevihane

Boğaziçi (Bosphorus)

Azapkapı Sokollu Mehmed Paşa Camii

Galata Kulesi (Galata Tower)

İstanbul Modern

PERŞEMBE PAZARI PARKI

KARAKÖY

Karaköy Meydanı

Galata Köprüsü (Galata Bridge)

GALOĞLU

Rüstem Paşa Camii (Rüstem Paşa Mosque)

Yeni Camii (New Mosque)

Eminönü Meydanı

SARAY BURNU

Mısır Çarşısı (Spice Market)

Sirkeci İstasyonu (Sirkeci Railway Station)

GÜLHANE PARKI

ymaniye ami

İstanbul iversitesi (İstanbul University)

E M İ N Ö N Ü

Topkapı Sarayı (Topkapı Palace)

ICAN

BEYAZIT

Arkeoloji Müzeri (Archaeological Museum)

State Library

Bâb-ı-Âli Camii

Bab-ı-Selam (Gate of Salutations)

Nuruosmaniye Camii

eyazıt Camii

Kapalı Çarşı (Grand Bazaar)

Bâb-ı-Âli

Aya İrini (Church of St Eirene)

azıt anı are)

Çemberlitaş (Column of Constantine)

Bab-ı-Hümayün (Imperial Gate)

Hagia Sophia (Aya Sophia)

Yeniceriler

Divan Yolu

Marmara Denizi (Sea of Marmara)

UMKAPI

Türk ve İslam Eserleri Müzesi (Museum of Turkish and Islamic Arts)

N

Sokollu Mehmed Paşa Camii (Sokollu Mehmed Paşa Mosque)

Sultan Ahmet Camii (Blue Mosque)

Cankurtaran İstasyonu (Cankurtaran Railway Station)

Istanbul

0   200   400   600   800   1000 m

Kennedy

(Sahil Yolu)

SULTANAHMET

Küçük Aya Sofya Camii

0   200   400   600   800   1000 yds

21

Sultanahmet and Kumkapı

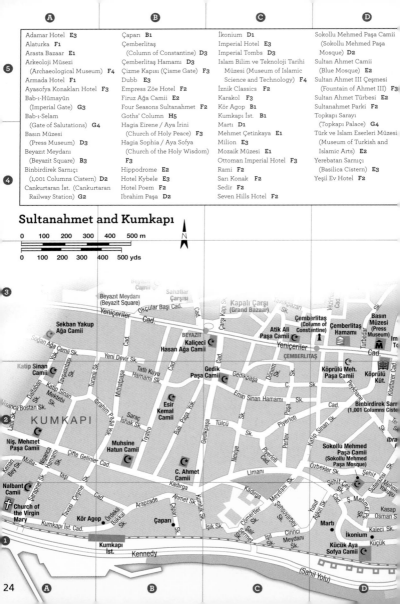

Glory in a **sultan's view of the Bosphorus** from the Iftar Canopy in the **Topkapı Palace**

If there's one place in Istanbul that no visitor should miss, it is the Topkapı Palace, the wonderful, romantic collection of kiosks and pavilions enclosed behind a high stone wall that was home to the Ottoman sultans from the 15th to the 19th century. It's here, standing beneath the Iftar Canopy in the Fourth Courtyard, where the sultans would have broken their fast on every day of Ramadan, that Turkish history will speak most loudly to you, relaying the stories of the powerful men and women who made the Ottoman Empire such a force to be reckoned with.

Gazing out from the Iftar Canopy towards the point where the Bosphorus meets the Sea of Marmara and the Golden Horn, you will be standing in one of the city's most historic spots, where the original Greek settlers established the colony that became Byzantium, where the early Byzantine emperors lived in splendour, and where Sultan Mehmed II ('the Conqueror') built his palace after conquering Constantinople in 1453.

The delicate Iftar Canopy was built in 1640 for Sultan İbrahim and stands between two lovely pavilions erected in the 1630s to celebrate Sultan Murad IV's conquests of Baghdad and Yerevan. Unlike his uncle Murad, İbrahim was a weak sultan who came to be nicknamed 'the Mad', not least because of his fondness for immensely fat women.

THE HAREM

Don't miss the wonderful Harem, the private quarters of the sultans from the late 16th century, where the sultans' wives and favourites lived, closely guarded by eunuchs.

HAGIA EIRENE

On the way out of the palace, pause to appreciate Hagia Eirene (Aya İrini), the huge brick-built Church of Holy Peace, which is contemporary with Hagia Sophia. Today, the only way to get a look inside at the breathtakingly expansive domed ceiling is by attending one of the classical concerts of the Istanbul Music Festival in June.

The finest rooms include the delicious Sultan's Hamam (Turkish Bath) and the Salon of Murad III, designed by the great Ottoman architect Sinan in 1578; the bright Pavilion of Sultan Ahmed I with gorgeous views; and the exquisite Fruit Room, decorated with frescoed flowers for the tulip-loving Sultan Ahmed III.

Other must-sees include the Treasury – three rooms full of treasure housed inside an old Turkish bath; the lovely Throne Room, where the sultan would have received foreign visitors; the Pavilion of the Holy Mantle, which houses holy relics brought to Istanbul by Sultan Selim I in 1517; and the Divan, where imperial business was conducted. Stop for lunch at the **Konyalı** (tel: 212-513 9696) or **Karakol** (tel: 212-514 9494) restaurants in the palace grounds.

Topkapı Palace (Topkapı Sarayı); www.topkapisarayi.gov.tr; Wed–Mon, summer 9am–7pm, winter 9am–5pm; charge, extra for the Harem; map G4

Treat yourself to a blowout **Sunday brunch** at the Sultanahmet prison turned **Four Seasons Hotel**

At the turn of the 20th century it would have been a grim presence brooding over the surrounding streets. Astonishingly, what is now the swish and fashionable Four Seasons Sultanahmet Hotel started life as Sultanahmet Prison, a huge holding-tank just around the corner from the Palace of Justice that stood over what is now the Sultanahmet Archaeological Park until it burnt down in 1933. The prison was especially notorious for housing political prisoners, among them the writers Nazım Hikmet and Yaşar Kemal. It also caged Billy Hayes, the drug-runner of *Midnight Express* infamy, in the early 1970s.

Every Sunday, residents and non-residents flock to avail themselves of what has to be one of the finest brunches in town. Eggs in every shape and size, sushi and sashimi, swordfish carpaccio, fresh honey and cream, handmade pasta, and a dessert spread so alluring it could qualify as a work of art – it's all here waiting to be savoured to the accompaniment of live jazz. Eating well doesn't come cheap, at a thumping TL99 per person. To keep the bills down, why not stop by for a delicious ice cream or afternoon tea instead?

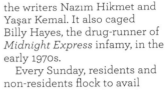

Alternatively, cross the road to the **Seven Hills Hotel** (Tevkifhane Sokak 8/A; tel: 212-516 9497). Breakfast in the rooftop restaurant may not match the Four Seasons' brunch for choice, but the magnificent views of Hagia Sophia and the Blue Mosque more than compensate.

Four Seasons Sultanahmet Hotel; Tevkifhane Sokak 1; tel: 212-638 8200; www.fourseasons.com; brunch served 11.30am–3pm; map F2

Mentally reconstruct the Byzantine Great Palace from the stunning **tesserae of the Mosaics Museum**

In the 1930s, workers toiling away near the Arasta Bazaar *(p.31)* were startled to find themselves gazing down on a huge stretch of mosaic. It was the first major piece of the Byzantine Great Palace to be unearthed and is still the most visually stunning. Today, more and more evidence of the palace is coming to light in the area that stretches from Hagia Sophia down to the Sea of Marmara. As it does so, archaeologists are building a better picture of the extraordinary collection of mansions that together formed a palace not dissimilar to the later Topkapı. For most casual visitors, however, the giant mosaic, preserved *in situ*, remains the easiest piece of the jigsaw to understand.

The mosaic turned out to be made up of some 75–80 million coloured tesserae (mosaic pieces), showing a series of scenes set against a white background. Look closely and you'll be able to make out children herding ducks, a monkey trying to catch birds, and even a bear up a tree. Not far from the entrance, two children are playing with a hoop, a seemingly innocent scene that may actually have had a political message, with the colour of their clothes intended to remind onlookers of the Greens and Blues, the hugely popular chariot teams whose football-hooligan-like followers burnt down the original Hagia Sophia during a riot.

Great Palace Mosaics Museum (Mozaik Müzesi); Torun Sokak; tel: 212-518 1205; Tue–Sun, summer 9am–6.30pm, winter 9am–4.30pm; charge; map E1

29

Dodge the tour parties and **approach the Blue Mosque from the Hippodrome** as originally intended

With its six pencil-thin minarets arising from a nest of domes, the Blue Mosque is an icon of Istanbul, its silhouette one of the most striking features of the skyline. The mosque was built for Sultan Ahmed I between 1609 and 1616, and takes its name from the quantity of predominantly blue İznik tiles with which it is decorated.

SULTAN AHMED

Sultan Ahmed I ascended the throne at the age of 12 and reigned from 1603 to 1617, dying at just 27. He was a deeply religious man with a love of writing poetry, which he penned under the name of Bahti. His wife, Köşem Sultan, was one of the most powerful women in the Ottoman state; she ruled the Harem and (historians suggest) the empire for nearly 50 years through her husband, two sons and grandson Mehmed IV.

Architect Sedefkar Mehmed Ağa designed the mosque to be approached via the Hippodrome, so do yourself a favour and ignore the more obvious (and crowded) entrance facing Hagia Sophia and approach from what feels like the side. Don't forget to remove your shoes before entering. Women should also cover their heads, shoulders and legs.

THE HIPPODROME

Originally planned to stage the popular chariot races that were a feature of Byzantine life, the Hippodrome retains several important monuments, including the fountain donated to the city by Kaiser Wilhelm II in 1898, an obelisk brought from Thebes that rests on a Byzantine plinth, the remains of a bronze cauldron supported by three snakes, and a second obelisk – the so-called Knitted Column – in a poor state of repair since the Fourth Crusaders stole its metal cladding in 1204.

To see the Blue Mosque at its floodlit best, book a window table at **Rami** (Utangaç Sokak 6; tel: 212-517 6593; map F2), across the road inside a restored wooden house.

Blue Mosque (Sultan Ahmet Camii); daily, avoid prayer times; map E2

Shop for the **perfect souvenir** in the classy **Arasta Bazaar**

Traditionally, many mosques took their running costs from the profits made by shops attached to them. These attached shops were called *arastas*. The Arasta Bazaar attached to the Blue Mosque is now a delightful, up-market passage lined with small shops selling carpets, kilims, felt products, ceramics, jewellery, antiques and towels. It is a much quieter, calmer place to shop than the Grand Bazaar *(p.52)*, but to make the most of it you still need to set aside some time to compare prices and perhaps bargain a little with the shopkeepers.

Cocoon (93) made a name for itself selling new-wave felt products, which include colourful caps and shawls so fine it's hard to credit that they're made from compressed wool. **Jennifer's Hamam** (135) sells handwoven towels and textiles from all over Turkey, as well as rose-scented toiletries. **Ata Ceramic** (57) offers İznik quartz ceramics made by Kütahya craft workers. **Motif Nomadic Art** (77) retails a variety of pieces left over from the days when many Turks lived a nomadic lifestyle, their women working at beautiful weavings merely to store such day-to-day items as salt or rolling pins. **Meerschaum Pipes** (63) sells pipes of such complexity they could only be ornamental, made from meerschaum mined at Eskişehir in Western Anatolia.

Arasta Bazaar; map E1, E2

Follow in the footsteps of the Ottoman viziers on a **stroll along Divan Yolu**

Every day thousands of tourists stroll up and down the road beside the Sultanahmet tramline without realising that they are following in the footsteps of the viziers who were responsible for running the Ottoman Empire as they headed for weekly meetings in the Council Chamber (Divan) of Topkapı Palace. Divan Yolu is jam-packed with minor historic monuments that often go overlooked amid the restaurants and souvenir shops.

Start your walk beside the entrance to the Basilica Cistern (*right*), where a marble stump is all that remains of the Milion, a monument from which distances used to be measured in Roman times. Walking up Divan Yolu, you will see on the left the exquisite, small Firuz Ağa Mosque from

1491. In the park behind it are the scant remains of the mansions of two Byzantine noblemen.

A little further up the road on the right, a large graveyard contains the tombs of sultans Mahmud II (1808–38), Abdülaziz (1861–76) and Abdülhamid II (1876–1909). Across the road is a small brick library dating back to 1661 and paid for by the Grand Vizier Mehmed Paşa and his son Fazıl Ahmed Paşa.

On the right-hand side of the road is the Press Museum where old printing presses are preserved inside a fine 19th-century apartment block. Then you will arrive at Çemberlitaş, where Divan Yolu becomes Yeniçeriler Caddesi.

Divan Yolu; map D3, E2

Enjoy an **atmospheric concert** in the underground **Basilica Cistern**

Just steps away from Hagia Sophia *(pp.34–5)*, the Basilica Cistern is an awe-inspiring underground reservoir in which 336 columns, some of them boasting fine carved capitals, support a vaulted roof beneath which visitors can wander round on walkways and gaze down at the fish flickering through the water, before pausing to snap the famous upside-down head of Medusa reused as a column base. It's one of the most impressive reminders of a complex system of aqueducts and reservoirs that kept the Byzantine city supplied with water.

In summer, look out for notices in the entrance to the cistern advertising concerts that take place on a platform suspended over the water. It is an extraordinarily atmospheric setting for music. And if you are lucky, you might catch a concert by the Mehter Band, the Ottoman marching band whose music inspired Mozart among others.

If the cistern catches your imagination, you could also visit the **1001 Columns (Binbirdirek) Cistern** (İmran Öktem Caddesi; daily 10am–6pm; charge; map D2), a short walk up Divan Yolu, or even make a reservation for dinner in a cistern at the **Sarnıç (Cistern) Restaurant** (tel: 212-512 4291; map F3), in lovely Soğukçeşme Sokak beside the Topkapı Palace.

Basilica Cistern (Yerebatan Sarnıçı), Yerebatan Caddesi; tel: 212-522 1259; Tue–Sun, summer 9am–6.30pm, winter 9am–5.30pm; charge; map F3

Take a bird's-eye peek at **Hagia Sophia's glorious mosaics** from the upper galleries

Of all Istanbul's great glories, perhaps the finest is Hagia Sophia (Holy Wisdom), the enormous domed church built by the Byzantine Emperor Justinian between 532 and 537, which survived the vicissitudes of history to become the Aya Sofya Mosque after the Ottoman conquest in 1453.

Although no one would want to leave Hagia Sophia without walking round its sprawling nave, a great way to escape the crowds is to slip upstairs to the galleries, where, in any case, many of the best mosaics are to be found.

At the top of the stairs turn right and walk along the gallery facing the altar from where the empress is thought to have watched services. The gallery then runs above the south aisle, divided in two by a screen that imitates in marble the appearance of a wooden door. Beyond this, on the right, is a superb mosaic showing Christ between Mary and John the Baptist (*pictured on pp.14–15*). It is regarded as one of the finest works of the Renaissance that took place after the Byzantine Emperors recovered the city from its Latin occupiers in 1261.

At the end of the gallery are two more fine mosaics: the Emperor John Comnenus (1118–43), his wife Eirene and their son Alexius praying to the Virgin Mary *(pictured)*; and Christ blessing the Emperor Constantine IX Monomachos (1042–55) and his wife Zoë. From here, gaze down into the apse for the best view of the dazzling mosaic of the Virgin.

Before walking round to the opposite gallery, peep over the balustrade to inspect mosaics in the nave of the saints Ignatius the Younger, John Chrysostom and Ignatius Theophorus which are invisible from ground level. One last mosaic high up on a column in the far gallery depicts the brutal Emperor Alexander (912–13).

GROUND LEVEL

Back at ground level, look for the circle of coloured marble set into the floor that marks the spot where the Byzantine emperors used to be crowned. You may also wish to queue to rotate your finger in a 'weeping' hole in one of the columns. Be sure to examine two more fine mosaics, one over the main entrance showing an enthroned Christ and prostrated Leo the Wise (886–912), the other above the exit door depicting the Virgin Mary and Christ Child with Constantine offering them a model of the city and Justinian offering a model of the church.

Finally, don't forget to pop round the corner and use the side entrance to visit the newly opened tombs of some of the 16th- to 18th-century sultans. That of Sultan Murad III also contains the tombs of his 19 sons, murdered on the same day in 1595 to ensure the smooth succession of Mehmed III.

Hagia Sophia (Aya Sofya); Tue–Sun, summer 9am–7.30pm, winter 9am–5pm; charge; map F3

35

Whip up a tasty **Turkish lunch** at the **Alaturka cookery school**

Turkish cuisine is widely regarded as one of the best in the world, so where better to try your hand at cooking it yourself than Istanbul, where so many of the finest dishes were originally designed to tempt the palates of the sultans? If you are already tiring of routine shish kebabs, this will also be an opportunity to rediscover the rich variety of traditional Turkish cookery.

In the backstreets of Sultanahmet, Alaturka is a small, privately owned cookery school where groups of up to a dozen foodies are taught the basics of how to prepare a five-course lunch by Dutch-born Eveline Zoutendijk and Mersin-born Feyzi Yıldırım on a half-day course. This is a very hands-on cooking experience, with group members joining in with every stage of food preparation. Typically, you will learn to prepare such popular dishes as *yayla çorbası* (pasture soup – a yoghurt-based starter), *kabak mücveri* (zucchini pancakes), *karnıyarık* ('split belly' – a stuffed aubergine main course) and *incir dolması* (delectable stuffed figs).

Afterwards, what could be more enjoyable than sitting down with your fellow chefs to tuck into your own handiwork, along with a good bottle of Turkish wine?

Private tours of the Spice Market *(p.88)* to shop for lunch ingredients can also be arranged.

Cooking Alaturka; Akbıyık Caddesi 72A; tel: 212-458 5919; www.cooking alaturka.com; charge; map F1

Count the tulips on the **İznik tiles** in the
Sokollu Mehmed Paşa Mosque

In the 16th century, the small lakeside town of İznik to the southeast of Istanbul became the centre for the production of exquisite ceramics, particularly tiles. What made these tiles so special was not just that they were fabricated from up to 80 percent quartz, but also the fact that the ceramicists had mastered the tricky business of producing the bright tomato red that came to be known as Armenian bole. İznik tiles crop up in many of Istanbul's most important mosques, including the Blue Mosque, as well as in the Topkapı Palace where they were used to decorate the Salon of Murad III.

To admire some beautiful but little-visited İznik tiles, wander downhill behind the Hippodrome and explore the spectacular Sokollu Mehmed Paşa Mosque,

built in 1571 for the Grand Vizier Sokollu Mehmed Paşa by the great Ottoman architect Sinan. Look out in particular for the images of pointy-petalled tulips, a flower shape particularly revered by the sultans. They are high up on the walls.

After a long period in the doldrums, İznik tiles are now being manufactured again, although the highest-quality tiles inevitably fetch premium prices. **İznik Classics** (Utangaç Sokak 17; map F2) is one dealer that specialises in the sale of İznik tiles, as well as a range of traditional and contemporary ceramics.

Sokollu Mehmed Paşa Mosque; Şehit Mehmet Paşa Yokuşu, Suterazisi Sokak, Kadırga; daily but avoid prayer times; map D1, D2

Relax over a sugary **Turkish coffee** in the **Museum of Turkish and Islamic Arts**

Overlooking the Hippodrome (*p.30*) is a marvellous brick mansion, the last remaining private 'palace' to survive from the 16th century and home at one time to İbrahim Paşa, a favourite of Sultan Süleyman the Magnificent. Today, it houses the magnificent Museum of Turkish and Islamic Arts, where you can inspect wonderful old carpets so long that they stretch from floor to ceiling, as well as all sorts of delicate ceramics, Qur'an stands, candlesticks and mosque lamps. Downstairs in the basement you can also find out more about the nomadic lifestyle once followed by many Turks, as well as admire reconstructions of house and shop interiors.

Visitors are often so wrapped up in the exhibits that they forget to leave time for a coffee in the cute little Ottoman café in the museum grounds. A peaceful haven from the hurly-burly outside, this is a great place to get to grips with a coffee 'alaturka'.

Nowadays, when tea is king, it's sometimes hard to remember that coffee was once the Turkish tipple of choice. But this was no wimpish cappuccino or latte. Instead, it was full-throttled coffee served in a tiny porcelain cup that allowed for just a couple of swigs before you hit the grains. Want to try it? Then the vocab you need is as follows:

şekersiz – no sugar
az şekerli – a little sugar
orta şekerli – medium sugar
çok şekerli – lots of sugar

Museum of Turkish and Islamic Arts (Türk ve İslam Eserleri Müzesi); At Meydanı; tel: 212-518 1805; Tue–Sun 9am–4.30pm; charge; map E2

Learn about the **antique carpet trade** on a visit to the **Mehmet Çetinkaya Gallery**

At the very first mention of Turkey your thoughts might well turn to oriental carpets. The trouble is that if you don't know anything about rugs, it will be hard to separate the true carpet lovers from those who just see dollar signs. Before you make any purchases, you would be well advised to have a good look around, and where better to start than in the gallery of renowned collector Mehmet Çetinkaya?

Çetinkaya specialises in carpets and textiles from Central Asia, and is well known for his stunning and colourful *kaitag* embroideries from Daghestan. Here, too, you will find rich, heavy Uzbek velvets as well as thick denim-blue quilts from Iran, cute little embroidered skullcaps and ready-made *chapans* (cotton robes).

Those whose budgets don't stretch to collectors' prices might prefer to seek out **Sedir** (Mimar Mehmed Ağa Caddesi 37; map F2), a four-storey carpet emporium standing right over the remains of a medieval chapel complete with sacred spring. Alternatively, **Şişko Osman** (Zincirli Han 15) in the Grand Bazaar not only has a well-deserved reputation for the quality of his products, but also boasts a shop in one of the bazaar's prettiest corners.

Best buys? Fast-vanishing nomadic pieces, such as opened-out camel bags, woven baby's cradles, and *sofras* (dining cloths), are among the more interesting pieces to look for.

Mehmet Çetinkaya Gallery; Tavukhane Sokak; tel: 212-517 6808; www.cetinkayagallery.com; also in the Arasta Bazaar (151); map E1

Go **birdwatching** for parakeets and herons in beautiful **Gülhane Park**

What is now Gülhane Park was once the outer reaches of the Topkapı Palace gardens. This lovely open space, in an often-crowded city, is best visited in spring when the flowerbeds will be radiant with tulips.

However, no matter what time of year you visit, you will always be able to appreciate the birdlife in the park. In summer the shrill cry of green parakeets cuts the air, interspersed with the cackle of jackdaws and the mournful cry of seagulls. But in winter, when the trees are bare, you will be able to appreciate the vast heronry that fills the branches on the west side of the park. Who knows how long they have been there, but sultans' turbans were often decorated with herons' feathers, so it could have been for a very long time.

A stroll around the park should bring you to the Goths' Column, which dates back to the 3rd or 4th century. Nearby, a row of tea gardens roll out the samovars to encourage visitors to linger and soak up a spectacular view of the confluence of the Bosphorus and the Sea of Marmara.

Gülhane Park; map F4

> **MUSEUM OF ISLAMIC SCIENCE AND TECHNOLOGY**
> The newly opened Museum of Islamic Science and Technology (Fri–Wed 9am–4.30pm; charge; map F4) is full of interesting data about past Middle Eastern scientific prowess. Many of the models on display are modern replicas, but the gorgeous ceiling paintings alone justify the admission fee. You don't even have to go inside to inspect the globe outside that depicts the world as shown on a 16th-century map.

Wonder at the ancient tiled lions and latest excavation finds in the **Istanbul Archaeological Museum**

Immediately downhill from Topkapı Palace is the Archaeological Museum. Like the British Museum, it's a treasure-chest not just of artefacts from all around Turkey but also from further-flung parts of the Ottoman Empire. One of the most prized possessions is the glorious Alexander Sarcophagus, excavated from a necropolis in Sidon (Lebanon). The Museum of the Ancient Orient in the same grounds also houses wonderful tiled lions (*pictured*) brought from Baghdad, as well as the Kadesh Treaty, an early peace treaty on clay drawn up between the Hittites and Egyptians in 1269 BC.

The most exciting recent additions to the museum are the finds made during the course of excavations to create a tunnel under the Bosphorus as part of the Marmaray traffic reduction project. The exhibits are mainly small homely items found in Üsküdar, Eminönü and the grounds of the Four Seasons Sultanahmet Hotel (*p.28*), but breathtaking photographs reveal the extraordinary discovery of the remains of 34 medieval ships, dating from the 5th to 11th centuries, which were found complete with their cargoes at the site of the Byzantine and Ottoman port in Yenikapı.

Standing in the museum grounds is a delightful tiled pavilion, the Çinili Köşk, from the reign of Sultan Mehmed II.

Archaeological Museum; Osman Hamdi Bey Yokuşu; tel: 212-520 7740; Tue–Sun 9am–5pm; charge; map F4

Let the gypsy musicians serenade you over a
fish supper in bustling Kumkapı

Kumkapı is a run-down suburb just inside the ruins of the sea walls that once protected the historic peninsula from assault from the Sea of Marmara. Once home to a large Greek and Armenian population, it is fast succumbing to tourism as real-estate prices force would-be hoteliers out of nearby Sultanahmet. But Kumkapı has always been known as a place to come for a lively night out at a fish restaurant, a legacy of its non-Muslim heritage.

Every night in summer the tables are dragged out into the main square and life morphs into one big party as gypsy musicians wander from one table to another serenading diners. Their attentions don't come free – when a musician points his clarinet at a diner the expectation is that they will stuff banknotes into it.

The fishing fleet still sets sail from Kumkapı on a daily basis, which means that the fish here should be as fresh as it comes. For the best prices – and arguably the freshest fish – you should actually cross over the busy Sahil Yolu (Coast Road) to dine at the newer restaurants that have opened right by the harbour.

A word of warning. Fish is one of the rare Turkish food products where the price is unregulated. Scams are not unknown, so always check the price of everything carefully and send back anything you didn't order. And never leave handbags dangling from the back of chairs.

Restaurants worth frequenting? **Kör Agop** (Blind Agop; Ördekli Bakkal Sokak 7; tel: 212-517 2334; map B1) and **Çaparı** (Çaparı Sokak 22; tel: 212-517 7530; map B1) are long-standing favourites.

Learn about **marbling, felt-making and *yazma*-printing** around Küçük Aya Sofya

Hagia Sophia may scoop all the publicity when it comes to Istanbul's early Byzantine churches, but in fact the Emperor Justinian had already sponsored the building of another elegant church dedicated to Saints Sergius and Bacchus in 527. It was converted into a mosque called **Küçük Aya Sofya** (Little Aya Sofya) in 1453 and, although its mosaics are sadly no longer in place, this is still one of the city's prettiest buildings, with a unique rotunda of marble columns supporting a matching upper gallery.

The cells of the *medrese* (theological school) attached to Küçük Aya Sofya house small crafts workshops where *ebru* artists often work. Currently very fashionable, *ebru* is the art of marbling paper by floating dye on the surface of water and then placing paper carefully on top to absorb the pattern.

The streets surrounding the mosque are starting to fill up with ateliers where you can watch miniature artists going about their art. Here, too, are the workshops of two people who are trying to revive traditional arts that had almost died out. At **Ikonium** Mehmet Gırgıç produces modern felt rugs and wall hangings as well as the traditional tall hats worn by the whirling dervishes. At **Martı** (Seagull), Veliye Marti is using *yazma* (woodblock) printing techniques to produce delightful contemporary cushion covers and wall hangings (*pictured*).

Ikonium; Küçük Ayasofya Caddesi 80/2; tel: 532-698 2824; www.thefeltmaker.net; Martı; Küçük Ayasofya Camii Sokak 12/A; tel: 212-458 5164; map D1

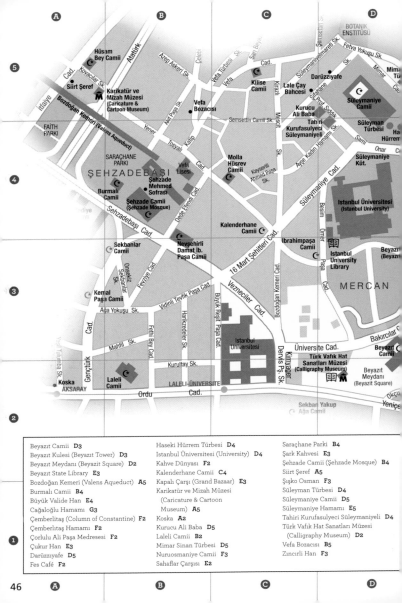

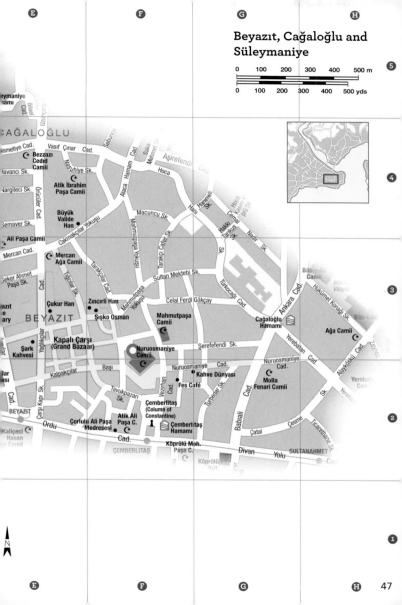

CAĞALOĞLU

smetiye Cad.

Vasıf Çınar Cad.

Bezzazı Cedid Camii

lavancı Sk.

Nasuhiye Sk.

Saka Mehmet Sk.

Aşirefendi Cad.

Hoca

Atik İbrahim Paşa Camii

largileci Sk.

Örücüler Cad.

Alaca Hamam Cad.

Macuncu Sk.

Hammeli Sk.

Hanı

Hakkı Tarsus

Cemal

Nadir Sk.

Büyük Valide Han

Çakmakçılar Yokuşu

Semaver Sk.

Ali Paşa Camii

Mercan Cad.

Mercan Ağa Camii

Tığcılar Sk.

Tarakçılar Cad.

Mahmutpaşa Yokuşu

Tarakçılar Sk.

Sultan Mektebi Sk.

Türkocağı Cad.

Celal Ferdi Gökçay

Bâb-ı Âli Camii

Hükümet Konağı Sk.

İstiklal Vilayet

Bâb-ı Âli

Şeker Ahmet Paşa Sk.

Cad.

azıt

ary

Çukur Han

Zincirli Han

Şişko Osman

BEYAZIT

Mahmutpaşa Camii

Cağaloğlu Hamamı

Ankara Cad.

Yerebatan

Ağa Camii

Alayköşkü Cad.

Zeytin

3

Şark Kahvesi

Yağlıkçılar

Kapalı Çarşı (Grand Bazaar)

Nuruosmaniye Camii

Şerefefendi Sk.

Nuruosmaniye Cad.

Yerebatan Camii

ar

ası

Çarşı Kapı Sk.

Kalpakçılar

Başı

Vezirhan Cad.

Nuruosmaniye Cad.

Kahve Dünyası

Molla Fenari Camii

Turbedar Sk.

Sk.

Yerebata

Çeşme

2

BEYAZIT

Tavukpazarı Sk.

Fes Café

Kaliçeci Hasan a Camii

Çorlulu Ali Paşa Medresesi

Atik Ali Paşa C.

Çemberlitaş (Column of Constantine)

Çemberlitaş Hamamı

Babıali Cad.

Çatal

Ticarethane Sk.

Ordu

Cad.

ÇEMBERLİTAŞ

Köprülü Mah. Paşa C.

Köprülü Küt

Divan

Yolu

SULTANAHMET

Cad.

1

N

Soak up the peace in the **quiet courtyard** of the great **Beyazıt Mosque**

When it comes to Istanbul's mosques, Sinan's is normally the name to conjure with. The beautiful Beyazıt Mosque that stands right beside the Grand Bazaar was, however, designed by an earlier architect, Yakub-şah ibn Sultan-şah, believed to have been Turkish despite his Persian-sounding name. Taking Hagia Sophia as his model, he supervised the construction of the mosque between 1501 and 1506, which means that Sinan would have been able to copy some of his best ideas.

The area beside the Grand Bazaar (p.52) is always very busy not just with shoppers but also with students heading for Istanbul University, which overlooks the main square. There are a couple of tea gardens where you can sit

down to watch all the activity, but for a few minutes of real peace and quiet the mosque's courtyard, with its graceful marble arcades and lovely ablutions fountain, is the perfect place to hide away. Afterwards, pop into the adjoining graveyard and inspect the tomb of Sultan Beyazıd II himself.

The creation of Beyazıt Square effectively destroyed the mosque complex. Today, the soup kitchen and caravanserai house the Beyazıt State Library, while the *medrese* on the far side of the square houses a Museum of Calligraphy. The hamam was crudely restored but has not yet reopened.

Beyazıt Mosque; map D2, D3

ISTANBUL UNIVERSITY

The giant Moorish gateway on the northern side of Beyazıt Square is the entrance to Istanbul University (Istanbul Üniversitesi), which houses in its grounds the Beyazıt Tower (Beyazıt Kulesi), an 85m-high stone structure, which was erected in 1828 as a lookout point for fires.

The university itself, founded at the time of the Ottoman Conquest, is the largest public university in Turkey, with around 60,000 students on its register. The Beyazıt Tower is not open to visitors, but you can usually take a stroll around the university grounds.

Browse for bargains at the **second-hand bookstalls** in the **Sahaflar Bazaar**

If you leave the Grand Bazaar by the Beyazıt Gate and then turn right, you will see on the left a small gateway that leads through into the Sahaflar Bazaar. Istanbul's best-known second-hand book market, its stalls clustered around a pretty central courtyard with a fountain and an army of cats. Once upon a time this really was a great place to search for second-hand books on a wide variety of topics. Nowadays, however, the proximity of Istanbul University just across the way means that most stallholders go for the easier pickings of selling textbooks to students, which is not to say that you won't find plenty of books about Turkey on sale here as well.

If second-hand books are your thing, look out for **Librairie de Pera** (Galipdede Caddesi 22), an Aladdin's cave of antiquarian books on all aspects of Turkey, Islam and the Middle East, which is the sole survivor of a whole row of bookshops at the Tünel end of İstiklal Caddesi. Alternatively, duck into the **Aslıhan Pasajı**, which runs off one side of the Balık Pazarı (p.108), itself just off İstiklal Caddesi. Here booths hawk all sorts of second-hand books and magazines at rather more down-to-earth prices.

Sahaflar Bazaar (Sahaflar Çarsısı); Cadırcılar Caddesi; Mon–Sat 9am–7pm; map E2

Bask in the luxury of a steamy **massage** in the historic **Cağaloğlu Hamam**

No one should leave Istanbul without paying a visit to a traditional hamam (hotel hamams don't count!). In the days before every house had its own plumbing, the hamams, or Turkish baths, played a major role in day-to-day life, with people frequenting them for a regular wash and brush-up as well as to celebrate high days and holidays.

Cağaloğlu Hamam is one of the best-known Turkish baths, not just because of the beauty of its architecture, but because many famous visitors to the city, including Florence Nightingale and Franz Liszt, used it. The routine here, as everywhere, is that you disrobe in an outer chamber and wrap yourself in a *pestemal*, a towel of strudel-like thinness. Inside the main chamber you fill a basin to your favoured temperature; it's a big faux pas to get soap in it. Most people opt to be scrubbed down with a *kese*, a glove with the texture of a cat's tongue, before enjoying a massage. Finally, you relax in the outer chamber over a glass of tea.

Other great baths worth trying include **Çemberlitaş Hamam** (Vezirhan Caddesi 8; tel: 212-522 7974; map F2) and the **Süleymaniye Hamam** (mixed bathing only; Mimar Sinan Caddesi 20; tel: 212-519 5569; map E5). Both were built by the Ottoman architect Sinan, and are great examples of a bathhouse built around a circular *sıcaklık*, where a domed roof pierced by tiny glass windows allows light to fall in shafts through the steam.

Cağaloğlu Hamam; Yerebatan Caddesi, Cağaloğlu; tel: 212-522 2424; www.cagaloğluhamami.com.tr; daily 8am–8pm; map G3

Wonder at a **skyline of domes and minarets** from the roof of the **Büyük Valide Han**

The ever-present skyline of Old Istanbul, a roller-coaster of domes and minarets, is one of its incidental pleasures, whether you are rumbling across the Galata Bridge in the tram or taking a ferry to almost anywhere. But there are still places in the city where the view is so spectacular that it takes your breath away, and one such place is the roof of the Büyük Valide Han in Çakmakçilar Caddesi, one of the wonderful but crumbling old workplaces-cum-inns that can be found in the labyrinth of streets meandering uphill behind the Spice Bazaar.

The Büyük Valide Han (Large Queen Mother's Han) was built in 1651 for Kösem Valide Sultan. In its heyday it could accommodate some 3,000 traders. If you wander inside, you may eventually come across the door leading up to the roof – or someone who can lead you to it. The view up the Bosphorus, down the Golden Horn and across the Old City is simply unforgettable.

Other spectacular views can be had from in front of the Yavuz Sultan Selim Mosque in Fatih, or from the gardens of the Süleymaniye Mosque (pictured).

Büyük Valide Han; map E4

Be at the **Grand Bazaar at opening time** to appreciate its 4,000-odd shops without the crowds

Colourful, chaotic, exotic, noisy – take your pick of adjectives and it will almost certainly describe the Grand or Covered Bazaar (Kapalı Çarşı), the labyrinthine collection of shops, stalls and *hans* that has been at the heart of the Istanbul shopping experience since the 15th century when the foundation stones were laid by Sultan Mehmed the Conqueror in 1461.

As long ago as 1867, Mark Twain was already complaining about the importunate salesmen, and not much has changed in the last 140-odd years. One way to ensure that you can appreciate the bazaar in peace and quiet is to get there as soon as the gates open. There may be no great fanfare about the event, but at least you will be able to get your bearings before the crowds press in, not to mention having the chance to breakfast with the early-bird salesmen in the many hole-in-the-wall cafés that exist to serve the workers rather than the tourists. Be sure to use the Nuruosmaniye Gate on the southeastern side – by far the most visually impressive.

WHAT TO BUY
Locals come to the Grand Bazaar primarily to buy gold jewellery to give as gifts at wedding and circumcision parties, hence the long street of jewellery shops that runs from the Nuruosmaniye Gate across to the Beyazıt Gate. Trinkets to look out for include rope-like necklaces from Trabzon on the Black Sea and delicate filigree earrings from Midyat in the southeast.

The bazaar is also a great place to shop for fabrics, including the glittering, candy-striped *kurnu* material made in Gaziantep in Central Anatolia. Hidden in the backstreets, you will also find several shops staffed by men from Turkmenistan who import lovely wooden boxes in red and black, and felt figurines from Central Asia.

The Bedesten, the giant strongbox of a building that lies at the heart of the bazaar, is a great place to hunt for antiques. You can also scout out carpets and leather goods here, as well as the usual array of T-shirts, tea sets and other souvenirs.

In most of modern Turkey haggling has died a death. In the bazaar it lives on. The best bargains go to the best bidders. The byword must be caution.

Grand Bazaar or Covered Market (Kapalı Çarşı); Ordu Caddesi, Beyazıt; Mon–Sat 9am–7pm; map E3; for refreshment options in and near the bazaar, see p.55

THE HANS

Travelling salesmen used to arrive in town with their pack animals and expect to put up for the night in digs close to their produce. The network of *hans* that catered for them was the urban equivalent of rural caravanserais, and some of the bazaar's most picturesque pockets remain the surviving *hans*, devoid of camels these days but with small businesses still ringing their courtyards. Most of the *hans* lie on the fringes of the bazaar. Particularly impressive examples include the İç Celebi and Zincirli *hans*; the latter is home to **Şişko Osman**, one of the bazaar's most prominent carpet dealers *(p.39)*. In quiet Çukur Han you can find **Nurem Art Textile**, which specialises in handwoven rugs from Central Asia.

Take a look at the ancient **Çemberlitaş Column**, last reminder of the **Emperor Constantine**

Held together with rusted bands of iron, the Çemberlitaş Column, one stop up the tram line from Sultanahmet, may not look much but is one of the very oldest historic monuments in the city, dating back to the reign of Constantine the Great (*r.* 324–37), the emperor who made Byzantium the capital of the eastern half of the Roman Empire and who, by espousing Christianity on his deathbed, set the religious tone for the next thousand years.

Thirty-five metres tall, the column is a memorial to Constantine's changing of the city's name to Constantinople. Originally it was surmounted by a statue of the Emperor as Apollo which was replaced by a giant cross when it fell down in the 12th century. Supposedly Constantine buried several important relics beneath the column, including a piece of the True Cross and some pieces of bread left over from the miracle of the loaves and fishes. They are yet to be uncovered.

Emperor Constantine is depicted in a mosaic in the **Hagia Sophia** (*pp.34–5*), where he offers the Virgin Mary and Christ Child a model of the city (*pictured*).

Çemberlitaş is the best known of the city's columns, but in the Fatih district there is another impressive column, the **Kıztaşı** (Maiden's Stone, Kıztaşı Caddesi), named after the carving of the goddess Victory on its base but sometimes confused with a lost Column of Venus that was said to sway whenever a true virgin passed by.

Çemberlitaş Column; map F2

54

Put your feet up over a **cappuccino** at the fashionable **Fes Café**

Shopping in the Grand Bazaar may be fun but it can also be wearing. Never fear because pedestrianised Nuruosmaniye Caddesi is now wall-to-wall coffee houses where you can take the weight off your feet without having to worry about being overpowered by traffic fumes. Several of the big chains are represented here, as is the cheaper but just as cheerful Turkish chain **Kahve Dünyası** (Coffee World; Nuruosmaniye Caddesi 79; map F2).

After something more individual? Then turn down Ali Baba Türbe Sokak, a side street at the bazaar end, to find **Fes Café**, a super-stylish modern café featuring fresh cakes and

sandwiches alongside the coffee. Come here for a superb blend of the kitsch (Abba on the TV, a stuffed zebra head on the wall) and the cool (gladioli on the tables and a branch of the luxury towel emporium Abdulla's on the premises).

If you would rather have your coffee inside the bazaar, a great option is the traditional **Şark Kahvesi** (Oriental Coffeeshop), on the main north–south thoroughfare, where the nicotine-coloured walls (no smoking inside though) are clad with images of oil wrestlers and costumed pashas; the portable pumping machine hanging from the ceiling would have been hooked up to a water supply in case of fire.

Fes Café also has a smaller branch inside the bazaar (*pictured*) in a line-up with several competitors, all of them atmospheric, all of them tiny and all of them frenetically busy.

Fes Café; Ali Baba Türbe Sokak, Beyazıt, and Halıcılar Caddesi in the Grand Bazaar; www.fescafe.com; bazaar branch closed Sun; map F2
Şark Kahvesi; Yağlıkçılar Caddesi 134, Grand Bazaar; tel: 212-512 1144; closed Sun; map E3

Drop in on the little-visited **Kalenderhane Mosque**, a Byzantine church converted into a mosque

When it comes to Byzantine churches-turned-mosques Hagia Sophia/Aya Sofya scoops all the attention, but in fact the city is dotted with other lovely Byzantine churches that were converted into mosques after the conquest of 1453. Conversion actually did them a big favour since it meant that the fabric of the building was maintained –

you only have to pass by the ruins of St John of Studion, the hugely important Byzantine monastery in Samatya, to appreciate what might have happened otherwise.

One of the finest of the smaller church-turned-mosques is the 12th-century Church of Theotokas Kyriotisaa, which was renamed Kalenderhane Mosque after a particular group of dervishes who frequented it until Atatürk abolished the dervish orders in 1925. Like all these churches, the Kalenderhane was built of brick in the shape of a cross topped off with a dome. During the course of restoration, frescoes of St Francis of Assisi – some of the earliest known of the saint – were discovered. They have been removed to the Archaeological Museum but are sadly not on display.

This is an especially picturesque corner of the city with the church pressed up against a crumbling stretch of the Aqueduct of Valens in an area which retains many old wooden houses, some of them slowly undergoing renovation. Yet it's only a short walk from the Grand Bazaar.

Kalenderhane Mosque; 16 Mart Şehitleri Caddesi; map C4

Tuck into a mouth-watering *büryan* kebab lunch in the shadow of the **Aqueduct of Valens**

One of Istanbul's least missable monuments is the enormous Aqueduct of Valens (*pictured*), straddling busy Atatürk Bulvarı as it runs downhill from the Şehzade Mosque to the Golden Horn. Dating back to 375, the aqueduct was part of an immensely complex system that once channelled water into the city from Thrace.

In the lee of the aqueduct is a fascinating and colourful quarter of the city known variously as Kadınlar Pazarı (the Women's Market), the İtfaiye Çarşısı (the Fire Station Market) and Küçük Siirt (Little Siirt). It takes the latter name from the southeastern town of Siirt, whence hail many of its residents. Consequently, the shops here are filled with produce from eastern Turkey, including a fine array of cheeses and honeys, and curious doughnut-like rings

of dried bread (*tandır ekmeği*) that must be rehydrated before eating.

This area is a great place to come at lunch time, when restaurants will be dishing up hefty portions of *büryan kebab*, lamb that has been baked for several hours in a sealed pit oven before being chopped into small pieces and served on a bed of *pide* bread. To go with it, request a portion of *perde pilav* (veiled rice), which will have been cooked in a special pot along with raisins, almonds and pieces of shredded chicken.

The welcoming **Siirt Şeref** restaurant is almost close enough to touch the aqueduct and has a roof terrace with a superb view.

Aqueduct of Valens (Bozdoğan Kemeri); map A5, B4
Siirt Şeref; İtfaiye Caddesi 4; tel: 212-635 8085; daily B, L and D; map A5

Treat yourself to **olive-oil soap** from the *sebil* (fountain) attached to the **Laleli Mosque**

Laleli Mosque was the last hurrah of the large imperial mosque complexes that were built in the three centuries following the Ottoman conquest; grand mosques continued to be built right up to the end of the 19th century but none of them came with the complement of additional builings that had turned the earlier models into local social and welfare centres. Designed between 1759 and 1763, it was the work of Mehmet Tahir Ağa for Sultan Mustafa III.

Often overlooked, *sebils* formed an important part of many mosque complexes. They were fountains the size of small rooms with grilled windows through which drinks were dispensed to passers-by. Today, many have found new uses as shopping kiosks, cafés and even as a carpet shop. The lovely example attached to the Laleli Mosque is now a shop selling olive-oil products including some fine soaps. Most of the produce comes from around Ayvalık, a small town on the Aegean coast south of Troy.

Afterwards, walk a little further downhill to visit the Valide Sultan Mosque, built for Pertevniyal Valide Sultan, the mother of Sultan Abdülaziz, in 1871, and graced with an impressive array of fountains. Despite its prominence, the architect remains uncertain.

Laleli Mosque; Ordu Caddesi; map B2

Pleasure your taste buds at **Koska**, a temple to **Turkish sweets**

You won't be in Istanbul for long before realising that most people here have a very sweet tooth. This expresses itself most vividly in the sheer quantity of sugar cubes dunked into tea, but is obvious too in the large number of shops selling nothing but sweets. Not for nothing is Turkish delight *(p.93)* synonymous with the country, although there are all sorts of other treats to be discovered too.

Just downhill from the Laleli Mosque *(left)* is a branch of Koska, which has been in business for over a century and sells sweets in every imaginable form. What to start with? Well, *helva* is an obvious choice since in Turkey the word covers not just the familiar sesame treat but a multitude of other sins too. In winter there will be mugs of hot *helva* parked by the doorway, while inside you will find crispy white bracelets of *helva* studded with sesame seeds, and even what Turks call 'wet helva' (marzipan), here often thickly studded with walnuts. Hanging from the ceiling you will also see what look like jellied sausages, but are actually dried fruits preserved in a *pekmez* (grape juice) jelly. They are called *köme* and are a favourite on the Black Sea.

Turkey's biggest manufacturer of chocolate is Ülker, on sale everywhere. Real chocaholics should try Mabel, which has been on sale since 1947, or even the 'nostaljı çikolatası' (nostalgic chocolate), sold from hole-in-the-wall shops along İstiklal Caddesi.

Koska; Ordu Caddesi 242, Aksaray; tel: 212-513 8900; www.koska.com; map A2

Enjoy **lunch with the locals** in front of the **Süleymaniye Mosque**

If Sinan was the acknowledged master of Ottoman architecture, the Süleymaniye Mosque, the domes and minarets of which bestride the skyline like a colossus, is certainly his Istanbul masterpiece, a vast complex complete not just with the mosque itself but also with a hospital, a caravanserai (inn for travellers), several *medreses* (theological schools), a hamam and a soup kitchen. It was a world within a world, which at one time even boasted its own wrestling arena. This is where Sultan Süleyman chose to be buried along with his wife Roxelana in a pair of *türbes* (tombs) in a pretty graveyard that fills with roses in summer. Allow plenty of time to make sure of doing it all justice.

This is made easier by the fact that there are several small *lokantas* (Turkish-style cafés) right on site, lined up along a street that glories in the unlikely name of Tiryaki Carşısı (Addicts' Market), after the opium-sellers who used to haunt it. The mainstay of these places is *kuru fasulye* (basically, baked beans), a popular Turkish staple sold here at rock-bottom prices. Best known of the *lokantas* is **Tarihi Kurufasulyeci Süleymaniyeli** (11; tel: 212-513 6219; map D4), where you can sit outside in the sun and gaze on the mosque while eating your beans. If it's full, **Kurucu Ali Baba** (1/3; tel: 212-520 7655; map D5) is just as good.

Should your exploration of the mosque extend until evening, another option is to settle down to dinner in what was once the *imaret* (soup kitchen), a cloistered oasis that dishes up Ottoman cuisine in its **Darüzziyafe** restaurant (Şifahane Caddesi 6; tel: 212-511 8414; map D5). Finally, there's a delightful tea garden, the **Lale**, which is very popular with local students, shoehorned in between the caravanserai and the soup kitchen.

SINAN'S TOMB

Just a few steps away from the mosque is the neat little corner tomb of Sinan (1490–1588) himself, which is decorated with a fine bust of the man who was responsible for 42 mosques in Istanbul alone. Fine examples include the Rüstem Paşa, Sokollu Mehmed Paşa and Şehzade mosques.

INSIDE THE MOSQUE

The vast domed space of the Süleymaniye Mosque can seem curiously empty but it is worth focusing on the details, especially the stained-glass windows by a certain İbrahim the Drunkard, the fine İznik tiles and the wooden shutters inlaid with mother-of-pearl. Ongoing restoration means that visitors can only see small parts of the interior for the time being.

Süleymaniye Mosque; daily, avoid prayer times; map D5

Stroll around the **restored wooden houses** of the **Süleymaniye neighbourhood**

Though hard to believe now, Istanbul was once a town of wooden houses. Indeed, in 1911 the great Swiss architect Le Corbusier wrote of the city: 'Every dwelling is of wood... All the great buildings, mosques, temples, caravanserais, are of stone.' The result was inevitable. Over the centuries the city was racked by fire after fire until eventually in the late 19th century the authorities decided that in future even dwellings would have to be built in stone.

The result is that original wooden houses are increasingly hard to find, even along the shores of the Bosphorus. Starting in the 1980s, a conservation movement got into its stride, converting some of the surviving wooden buildings into chichi hotels – a fine example is the row of houses that makes up Soğukçeşme Sokak between Topkapı Palace and Hagia Sophia, where pastel houses form the Ayasofya Konakları hotel (*p.179*).

One of the best areas in which to see some of the ordinary wooden houses that are now being restored is Süleymaniye, the district around the great Süleymaniye Mosque. Here you will find wooden houses in all states of repair, from complete dereliction to new-pin glossiness. Start exploring in Kayserili Ahmed Paşa Sokağı where the conservation authorities have their headquarters.

Afterwards, perhaps look again at the Beyazıt Tower in the grounds of Istanbul University (*p.48*) and ponder its original role as a watch tower for treacherous flames.

Kayserili Ahmed Paşa Sokağı; map D4–5

Puff on a *nargile* in the atmospheric **Çorlulu Ali Paşa Medresesi**

Not so long ago the *nargile*, or water pipe, appeared to be on its last legs, favoured only by the sort of elderly men in flat caps who hung out in traditional teahouses. Then suddenly it steamed back into vogue again and nowadays you can hardly move for trendy cafés offering the chance to smoke a *nargile* at the same time as you drink tea and play a game of *tavla* (backgammon).

One of *the* most atmospheric places to do this is right on the continuation of Divan Yolu as it heads west towards the Grand Bazaar. The Çorlulu Ali Paşa Medresesi is all that remains of a mosque complex built in 1708 for a man who was grand vizier to the tulip-loving Sultan Ahmed III until he was beheaded. Today, its proximity to Istanbul University ensures a lively student clientele who rub shoulders with their more traditional elders and the handful of tourists who drop by to inspect the carpets on sale beneath the portico.

There are several tobacco flavours to choose from, although apple tends to be the most popular. If you'd like to master some Turkish nargilese, the glass bowl is a *gövde*, the tube that connects it to the tray on top is a *marpuç*, the tray is a *lüle*, and the plastic mouthpiece is a *sipsi*.

Çorlulu Ali Paşa Medresesi; Yeniçeriler Caddesi 35, Beyazıt; tel: 212-511 8853; daily until late; map F2

Wrap your lips round a **glass of bitter *boza*** as Atatürk once did at the **Vefa Bozacısı**

In the backstreets of Vefa, not far from the Süleymaniye Mosque, stands a quaint little café, where the *raison d'être* is the promotion of *boza*. *Boza* is a distinctively Turkish drink made from fermented barley, and is best drunk with a sprinkling of cinnamon and a handful of chickpeas. According to the famous travel writer Ibn Battuta, a version of *boza* was already available in the 14th century. However, it wasn't until 1876 that the Vefa Bozacısı opened its doors to bring the drink to a wider audience. The renown of the store was once so great that even Mustafa Kemal Atatürk, Turkey's first president, dropped by for a tasting. The glass he used is carefully preserved in a wall cabinet today.

Boza not to your liking? Well, the Vefa Bozacısı also serves a sweet grape drink called *şıra* which is more immediately palatable.

While in Istanbul you might also like to sample a couple of other unusual drinks. The first is *sahlep*, which is made from the crushed roots of wild orchids. It is a thick, comforting drink, consumed in winter as an alternative to cocoa. In the colder months it goes on sale even on the ferries.

Finally, there's *şalgam* which is much more of an acquired taste. *Şalgam* is made from turnip juice and is a favourite drink of the area around Adana on the south coast. It is sold from churns on the Eminönü waterfront if you fancy trying it.

Vefa Bozacısı; Katip Çelebi Caddesi 104/1; tel: 212-519 4922, www.vefa.com.tr; daily B and L; map B5

Dine like a sultan in a converted *medrese* in the grounds of the **Şehzade Mosque**

The Süleymaniye may be the best known of architect Sinan's many mosques, but just a short walk away the Şehzade (Crown Prince) Mosque is almost as spectacular, yet very much less visited. The complex was built in memory of Süleyman the Magnificent's son Mehmed, who died of smallpox in 1543, and was the first of the large imperial complexes on which Sinan worked. Unlike the Süleymaniye, which is hemmed in by other buildings, the Şehzade stands in a large garden, with a group of tombs including those of Mehmed and his brothers Cihangir and Mustafa in the corner.

The garden is ringed with buildings that once formed part of the mosque complex, and one of them, the *medrese*, has been converted into a delightful restaurant and tea garden. The Şehzade Mehmed Sofrası (Crown Prince Mehmed Restaurant) dishes up appropriately Turkish cuisine in rooms that were once the cells where students lived. In summer, it is just as nice to sit in the courtyard and sip a glass of tea as you ponder all those who passed through before you.

It could hardly be less like the grand Şehzade Mosque, but the cute little Burmalı Mosque just round the corner is also worth a look. Its spiral-decorated minaret is unique in the city and a collection of old Roman capitals adorns the columns of its porch arcade.

Şehzade Mehmed Sofrası; Şehzadebaşı Camii Avlusu; tel: 212-526 2668; www. sehzademehmed.com.tr; daily L and D; map B4

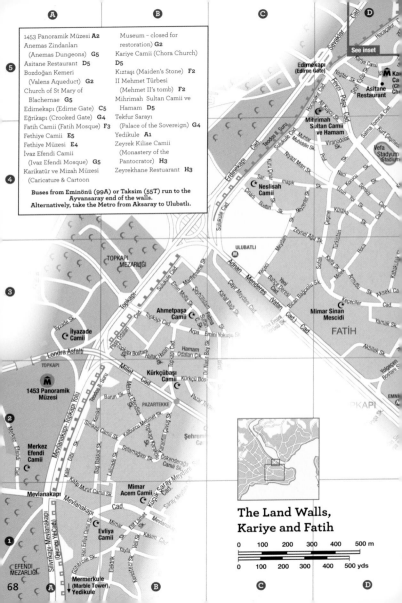

1453 Panoramik Müzesi **A2**
Anemas Zindanları
  (Anemas Dungeons) **G5**
Asitane Restaurant **D5**
Bozdoğan Kemeri
  (Valens Aqueduct) **G2**
Church of St Mary of
  Blachernae **G5**
Edirnekapı (Edirne Gate) **C5**
Eğrikapı (Crooked Gate) **G4**
Fatih Camii (Fatih Mosque) **F3**
Fethiye Camii **E5**
Fethiye Müzesi **E4**
İvaz Efendi Camii
  (İvaz Efendi Mosque) **G5**
Karikatür ve Mizah Müzesi
  (Caricature & Cartoon

Museum – closed for
  restoration) **G2**
Kariye Camii (Chora Church)
  D5
Kıztaşı (Maiden's Stone) **F2**
II Mehmet Türbesi
  (Mehmet II's tomb) **F2**
Mihrimah Sultan Camii ve
  Hamam **D5**
Tekfur Sarayı
  (Palace of the Sovereign) **G4**
Yedikule **A1**
Zeyrek Kilise Camii
  (Monastery of the
  Pantocrator) **H3**
Zeyrekhane Restuarant **H3**

Buses from Eminönü (99A) or Taksim (55T) run to the
Ayvansaray end of the walls.
Alternatively, take the Metro from Aksaray to Ulubatlı.

The Land Walls,
Kariye and Fatih

0   100   200   300   400   500 m

0   100   200   300   400   500 yds

68

Admire the crumbling towers and gates on a **walk** along the length of the ancient **Theodosian Walls**

As the taxi speeds you from the airport to the centre, you can hardly fail to spot the start of the incredible stretch of walls that protected Constantinople from invaders from 413 until 1204 when the Fourth Crusaders broke through. In 1453 Sultan Mehmed II put paid to any lingering sense of their invincibility with a little help from a Hungarian-made cannon called Urban.

In their heyday the land walls consisted of a double row of fortifications fronted by a 20m-wide moat. The walls were broken up by 81 gates, and there were 96 towers in both the inner and outer walls. The inner walls soared to a height of 12m, a size best appreciated at the Ayvansaray (northern) end, where several huge towers still survive virtually intact.

The walls we see today are an amalgam built up over the centuries, but most of the work is usually attributed to the Emperor Theodosius since the building commenced during his reign. Over the last decade or so, stretches of the wall have been restored or rebuilt, sometimes with a crudity that has been much criticised. Nevertheless, a walk along the walls remains enjoyable, despite the busy main road that now replaces the moat. It is best to wear good shoes, carry plenty of water and do the walk in company, since members of the heavy-drinking fraternity sometimes use the walls as a backdrop for their binges. The entire stretch of the walls extends for 6.5km, but it is perfectly easy to walk either from Yedikule to Topkapı or from Topkapı to Ayvansaray in a morning.

You can start at the Ayvansaray end of the walls on the Golden Horn, but most prefer to kick off at Memerkule (Marble Tower) on the

Sea of Marmara or a little further inland at Yedikule. The latter is a particularly good starting point as the surburban train line from Cankurtaran (Sultanahmet effectively) stops there.

As you walk along the walls you will see built into them many old stones that were clearly salvaged from an earlier structure, including lengthy inscriptions in Greek.

YEDIKULE

Memerkule originally stood right on the waterfront but is now marooned on a stretch of reclaimed foreshore. Beyond it, **Yedikule Hisarı** (Seven Towers Castle) was originally a group of four towers to which another three were added by Sultan Mehmed II so that they could act as a prison. Inside the grounds you will be able to make out the ghostly shape of the Golden Gate in the wall. Byzantine

emperors used to re-enter the city through this gate after military victories.

Close to the Ayvansaray end of the walls stands the Tekfur Sarayı (Palace of the Emperor), a restored late Byzantine palace building that went on to house a menagerie and then an 18th-century pottery maker. Although it has been restored to give an idea what it might have looked like in its heyday, it is not currently accessible.

Yedikule Hisarı; Kule Meydanı, Yedikule; daily 9am–6.30pm; charge; map A1; Tekfur Sarayı, map G4

Conjure up the noise and chaos of the Conquest of Istanbul at the **1453 Panorama Museum**

As 1066 is to British history, so 1453 is to Turkish history – one of those dates that everyone remembers because it marked such a decisive break with the past, in this case with the Byzantine past as the Ottomans under Sultan Mehmed II (nicknamed 'Fatih', the Conqueror) swept through the old Land Walls to seize the Christian city for Islam.

With the coming of the Turkish Republic in 1923, everything Ottoman fell from favour, even the Conquest. Now, however, Ottomania is very much of the moment, and with every passing year Istanbul celebrates the momentous events of 29 May 1453 with more and more verve.

One of the city's newest attractions is the 1453 Panorama

Museum near the Topkapı Gate in the land walls. Here you can walk around a giant 360-degree image of what happened on that day, complete with sound and light effects. The information panels lining the entrance are only in Turkish, but this is certainly somewhere to bring fractious children who are tiring of conventional museums and a surfeit of mosques.

To watch a reconstruction of the breaching of the walls, complete with brightly costumed Janissary soldiers, turn up at the Belgrade Gate around 10.30am on 29 May.

1453 Panorama Museum (1453 Panoramik Müzesi); Topkapı Gate; tel: 212-245 1453; www.panoramikmuze. com; daily 9am–5pm; charge; map A2

Get yourself a serious **scrub in the Mihrimah Sultan Hamam**, an under-visited work of Sinan

Like Rome, Old Istanbul was built on seven hills, and most of them were soon surmounted by impressive imperial monuments (Topkapı Palace stands on the first hill, while the Süleymaniye Mosque bestrides the third). The summit of the sixth and highest hill was the site of the Edirne Gate in the city walls, and just inside it architect Sinan created the magnificent Mihrimah Sultan Mosque for Sultan Süleyman the Magnificent's favourite daughter, Mihrimah. Completed in 1565, the mosque complex suffered terrible damage in later earthquakes but has just been completely restored.

For those prepared to venture a little off the tourist trail in search of authenticity, the hamam attached to the mosque is well worth visiting, especially as prices at the better-known baths

soar as high as a sultan's ransom. A double hamam, with separate sections for men and women as would have been normal in traditional society, the Mihrimah Sultan Hamam was restored in 2006, thereby guaranting squeaky cleanliness – not for nothing is the cockroach called the *hamamböceği* (hamam insect) in Turkish. The restoration added a small sauna cubicle as well as a band of beautiful turquoise tiles to the steam room. In the better-known hamams *(p.50)* you can sometimes find yourself having to wait a long time for your massage. Here you will be seen to at the double for a fraction of the cost.

Mihrimah Sultan Hamam; Fevzi Paşa Caddesi 333; tel: 212-523 0487; http:// mihrimahsultanhamami.com; daily 8am–7pm; map D5

Try **traditional dishes** celebrating the circumcision of an Ottoman prince at the **Asitane Restaurant**

Much of what is today described as Ottoman cuisine, as opposed to Turkish, was created to tempt the palates of the sultans and their entourage in the many-chimneyed kitchens of the Topkapı Palace. Palace food would never have been anything less than wonderful, but there were still special occasions when the chefs would pull out all the stops. These would include the *iftar* (break of fast) meals served every evening during Ramadan, but just as important were the parties held to celebrate the circumcisions of the sultans' sons. In Islamic countries boys are circumcised at about eight or nine, so the princes would have been old enough to appreciate the ceremony that went with the pain.

The Asitane Restaurant at the Kariye Hotel near the Chora Church *(p.76)* boasts a menu featuring dishes served at the party for Süleyman's sons Cihangir and Beyazıd in 1539. Fortunately, it omits the whole roasted cows stuffed with live rabbits and wolves that were supposedly served at the circumcision of Sultan Murad III's sons in 1582, going instead for unusual but mouth-watering dishes such as *badem çorbası* (almond soup), saffron rice with chickpeas, and *mutanjene* (diced lamb served with dried apricots, raisins, honey and almonds).

Asitane; Kariye Oteli, Kariye Camii Sokak 18; tel: 212-635 7997; daily L and D; map D5

Sip water from a sacred spring at a church that gave birth to a palace

They may not be immediately obvious, but Istanbul is pockmarked with sacred springs (*ayazmas*); at the last count more than 500 of them could still be identified, often in the grounds of 19th-century Greek and Armenian churches. The most important of all these springs was the one at Blachernae, close to the point where the land walls joined the sea walls at the Golden Horn.

Locations often remain sacred despite changes of religion, and thus it was that the spring at Blachernae, which was already attracting pilgrims in pre-Christian times, went on to become holy to Christians after the city capitulated to the new religion in the wake of the Emperor Constantine's conversion. A church was built at the site in 451, and it became a popular place of pilgrimage after it acquired clothing said to have been worn by the Virgin Mary that had been brought here from Jerusalem. In 627 the Blachernae incarnation of the Virgin was believed to have appeared to soldiers fighting to defend the walls against invading Avars. Regular visits to the spring became de rigueur, and it is thought that the Byzantine

emperors may have had the lost Blachernae Palace constructed nearby to accommodate them when they came to pray here.

Today, visitors to the 19th-century Greek Orthodox church of St Mary of Blachernae on the site can still drink water from the *ayazma*, just as the emperors did in years gone by.

St Mary of Blachernae Church (Blachernae Kilisesi); Ayvansaray Kuyu Sokak; daily 9am–6pm; map G5

Wonder at the **dramatic frescoes and mosaics** of the extraordinary **Chora Church**

Out on a limb near the Edirne Gate (Edirnekapı) in the land walls, the Chora Church (aka Kariye Mosque) has decor fabulous enough to compete with Hagia Sophia. A product of the Byzantine Renaissance that took place in the 14th century, when the emperor eventually managed to recover Constantinople from the Fourth Crusaders who had sacked it in 1204 and then installed a puppet government, this was paid for by one Theodore Metochites (1270–1332), a Byzantine statesman and poet who was advisor to Emperor Andronikos II Paleologos. In adorning an otherwise fairly ordinary 11th-century church with spectacular mosaics and frescoes, he turned what might otherwise have been an also-ran attraction into one of the city's finest sights.

THE FRESCOES

Most people are so stunned by the mosaics covering the ceiling of the narthex as they enter that they are already out of superlatives by the time they round the corner into the pareeclesion, or side chapel, and come face to face with the incredible frescoes emblazoning its walls and ceiling. Most dramatic are the images of mysterious Byzantine saints dressed in white robes adorned with black crosses, but the finest images are probably those of the *Harrowing of Hell* on the apse ceiling, and the *Last Judgement* in the centre of the ceiling, with heaven represented as what looks like a giant snail.

THE MOSAICS

Spectacular as the frescoes are, the mosaics can certainly give them a run for their money. Like the murals in medieval English churches, they retell Bible stories for the illiterate, albeit with a Byzantine twist that introduces, for example, a washerwoman to the traditional scenery of the Nativity.

As in Hagia Sophia, there are also several large set-piece mosaics, the most intriguing of which depicts Theodore Metochites kowtowing to Christ while sporting a hat so over the top that it would hardly look out of place at Ascot. Inside the nave – which is surprisingly modest, given the extravagant decor of the narthex and chapel – there are also fine images of Christ *(pictured)* and the Virgin Mary, as well as a scene of the Dormition of the Virgin above the entrance.

St Saviour in Chora Church (Kariye Camii); Kariye Camii Sokak, Edirnekapı; Thur–Tue 9am–5pm; charge; map D5

FETHIYE MUSEUM

So impressive is the Chora Church that you may feel you have already overdosed on mosaics. However, in high summer it can be very full with tour parties, in which case it's worth knowing about the Fethiye Museum (Fethiye Caddesi, Çarşamba; Thur–Tue 9am–5pm; small charge; map E4), a short walk east in the backstreets of Fatih. Here, a large 12th-century church has been split into two, with one part continuing in use as a mosque while the other serves as a museum, its walls and ceilings adorned with mosaics almost as fine as those of Chora but seen by only a rare handful of wanderers. Those lining the dome are a particular treat.

Hunt down a **secret cemetery** tucked inside the walls at **Ayvansaray**

In built-up modern Istanbul green space is always at a premium. In contrast, 19th-century writers rhapsodised about the sprawling rustic cemeteries that covered much of what is now the city centre. A huge cemetery, for example, straggled downhill from Taksim Square. Today, with the exception of a couple of walled cemeteries for non-Muslims in Şisli/Feriköy, most of the central graveyards have been redeveloped. The largest are now to be found at Eyüp on the Golden Horn and immediately across the road from the land walls at Merkezefendi.

There is, however, a particularly cute cemetery tucked up right inside the walls as they run downhill from Edirnekapı to the Golden Horn. The easiest way to find it is to enter the small park at Ayvansaray that surrounds the 17th-century Haci Hüsrev Mescid and then turn left towards the huge polygonal towers in the wall. Buried in the cemetery, which resembles a walled garden, are Ebu Ahmed El Ansari and Hamidullah El Ansari, said to have been companions of the Prophet Mohammed, as well as Toklu İbrahim Dede, thought to have taken part in the battle for the city in 1453. It's still a very holy site filled with people praying.

Cemetery of the Prophets' Companions; Ayvansaray; map G5

Admire a dramatic view of towers and unique wooden porticoes at the **İvaz Efendi Mosque**

Few visitors ever pause to explore the area just above the Ayvansaray end of the land walls, but were they to do so they would discover a traditional neighbourhood little changed in the last 50 years. The most conspicuous monument here is the İvaz Efendi Mosque, a large domed buildng with a single minaret that looks as if it should have been designed by Sinan. Rather surprisingly, it is not actually known who the architect was. Records suggest that it was built in the 1580s, but that is about all that is certain. Its most extraordinary features are the wooden porticoes that support the inside gallery (*pictured*). They hardly seem strong enough to bear the weight above them and are certainly unique in Istanbul.

The İvaz Efendi Mosque stands right beside the site of the Blachernae Palace where the later Byzantine Sultans lived after vacating the Great Palace in Sultanahmet, largely as a result of the damage done during the Latin Occupation (1204–61). Almost nothing remains of the palace now, although if you peer over the terrace of the İvaz Efendi Mosque you will see the Tower of Isaac Angelus II which formed part of it as well as the tower that houses the Dungeon of Anemas, a gloomy but atmospheric prison which is currently being restored.

İvaz Efendi Mosque; Dervişzade Caddesi; open around prayer times only; map G5

Relish **dinner with a view** in front of the **Monastery of the Pantocrator**

Neglected for far too long, the enormous red-brick, double-domed **Monastery of the Pantocrator** was restored in 2009 to form the centrepiece of a neighbourhood where work has also begun on renovating some of the old wooden houses. Converted into the Zeyrek Kilise Mosque in 1453, the monastery complex originally incorporated two churches and a mortuary chapel, all apparently built between 1120 and 1136 for one of the powerful Comneni emperors. It was so large and impressive that it was co-opted to serve as a theological school after the Conquest until the *medreses* ringing the new Fatih Mosque were completed.

Wonderful as the building is, the monastery is also worth visiting for its superb location on a bluff overlooking the Golden Horn, above the roaring traffic of bustling Atatürk Bulvarı. Taking advantage of the same views, the **Zeyrekhane Restaurant** (*pictured*) sits immediately in front of it, offering diners a wonderful panorama of the boats plying back and forth as they tuck into the house's own kebab or a tasty *piliç külbastı* (chicken cutlet). The menu draws on the Ottoman and Turkish repertoire but with a few international dishes thrown in to suit more conservative tastes.

Monastery of the Pantocrator; Tue–Sun 9am–5pm; Zeyrekhane Restaurant; İbadethane Arkası Sokak 10, Zeyrek; tel: 212-532 2778; daily L and D; map H3

Inspect the **tomb of the revered Sultan Mehmed the Conqueror** in the grounds of the **Fatih Mosque**

Although not much visited by tourists, the Fatih Mosque is one of Istanbul's most holy shrines, erected by Sultan Mehmed II ('the Conqueror') right over the site of the Church of the Holy Apostles, where many of the Byzantine emperors had been buried. Badly damaged by an earthquake in 1766, the mosque you see now is a mash-up of original work by Atik Sinan (not to be confused with the famous Mimar Sinan) and later work by Mehmed Tahir Ağa. Today, the huge mosque stands like a fortress at the heart of a conservative part of town, the *medreses* (theological schools) surrounding it erecting what looks like an all-but-impenetrable wall.

It's well worth exploring the mosque itself and the buildings that surround it. But to find the tomb of the Conqueror, you will have to wander into a walled graveyard beside the mosque. Here, Sultan Mehmed lies in a splendid *türbe* (tomb), usually full of pious well-wishers. Newly annointed sultans hurried here to pay their respects after strapping on the Sword of Osman at Eyüp *(p.140)*. Come here early in the morning on 29 May, the anniversary of the Conquest in 1453, to see the city bigwigs lined up to pay homage to him.

Fatih Mosque; Fevzi Paşa Caddesi; daily, avoid prayer times; map F2, F3

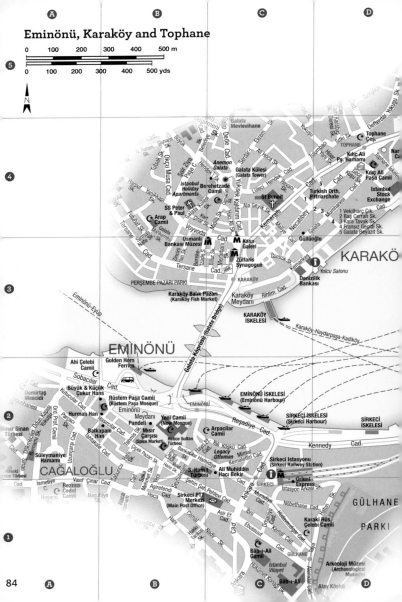

Eminönü, Karaköy and Tophane

0 100 200 300 400 500 m
0 100 200 300 400 500 yds

N

TOPHANE

Tophane Çeş.

Nar Cad.

Kılıç Ali Pş. Hamamı

Galata Mevlevihane Sk.

Kılıç Ali Paşa Camii

Turkish Orth. Patriarchate

Istanbul Stock Exchange

Okçu Musa Cad.

Anemon Galata

Galata Külesi (Galata Tower)

St Benoit

İstanbul Holiday Apartments

Berahetzade Camii

SS Peter & Paul

1 Vekilharç Çık.
2 Baş Cerrah Sk.
3 Kara Tavuk Sk.
4 Fransız Geçidi Sk.
5 Galata Beyazıt Sk.

Arap Camii

Galata

Voyvoda

Osmanlı Bankası Müzesi

Kasa Galeri

Güllüoğlu

KARAKÖ

Zülfaris Synagogue

KARAKÖY

Yolcu Salonu

PERŞEMBE PAZARI PARKI

Karaköy Balık Pazarı (Karaköy Fish Market)

Denizcilik Bankası

Karaköy Meydanı

Rıhtım Cad.

KARAKÖY İSKELESİ

Eminönü-Eyüp

Karaköy-Haydarpaşa-Kadıköy

EMİNÖNÜ

Ahi Çelebi Camii

Golden Horn Ferries

Galata Köprüsü (Galata Bridge)

Sobacılar Cad.

Demirtaş Mescidi

Büyük & Küçük Çukur Hans

Rüstem Paşa Camii (Rüstem Paşa Mosque)

EMİNÖNÜ İSKELESİ (Eminönü Harbour)

Hurmalı Han

Eminönü Meydanı

Balkapanı Han

Yeni Camii (New Camii)

Pandeli

S. Hamit Türbesi

Reşadiye Cad.

SİRKECİ İSKELESİ (Sirkeci Harbour)

SİRKECİ İSKELESİ

Mimar Sinan Türbesi

Süleymaniye Hamamı

Mısır Çarşısı (Spice Market)

Hatice Sultan Türbesi

Arpacılar Camii

Legacy Ottoman

Kennedy Cad.

CAĞALOĞLU

İsmetiye Cad.

Bezzazı Cedid Camii

Ali Muhiddin Hacı Bekir

Ankara Cad.

Sirkeci İstasyonu (Sirkeci Railway Station)

Orient Express

SİRKECİ

GÜLHANE

Haynacı

Nasuhiye

Sirkeci PTT Merkezi (Main Post Office)

Asır Ef. Cad.

Nöbethane Cad.

Karaki Hüs. Çelebi Camii

PARKI

Bâb-ı-Ali Camii

Istanbul Vilayet

İstanbul Vilayet

Arkeoloji Müzesi (Archaeological Museum)

Bâb-ı-Ali

GÜLHANE

Alay Köşkü

A   B   C   D

FINDIKLI
PARKI

Fındıklı Molla Çelebi Camii

Cihangir Camii

Mimar Sinan University

Mmar Sinan University

Boğazici

(Bosphorus)

Eminönü-Boğaz

Eminönü-Üsküdar

Sirkeci-Harem (Araba Vapurları) (Ferry Boat)

Eminönü-Kadiköy

SARAY
JRNU

Atatürk Heykeli

Gothe Column

Ali Muhiddin Hacı Bekir **C2**
Anemon Galata **C5**
Arap Camii **B4**
Balkapanı Han **B2**
Berehetzade Camii **C4**
Büyük & Küçük Çukur Hans **B2**
Eminönü Meydanı **B2**
Galata Köprüsü (Galata Bridge) **B3**
Galata Külesi (Galata Tower) **C4**
Golden Horn Ferries **B2**
Gülhane Parkı **D1**
Güllüoğlu **C3-4**
Hatice Sultan Türbesi **B2**
Hurmalı Han **B2**
Istanbul Holiday Apartments **B4**
Istanbul Modern **E4**
Istanbul Stock Exchange **D4**
Karaköy Balık Pazarı (Karaköy Fish Market) **B3**
Karaköy Meydanı **C3**
Legacy Ottoman Hotel **C2**
Mısır Çarşısı (Spice Market) **B2**
Nargile Cafés **D4**
Nusretiye Camii **E4**
Orient Express Restaurant **C1**
Pandeli **B2**
Rüstem Paşa Camii (Rüstem Paşa Mosque) **B2**
Sirkeci Istasyonu (Sirkeci Railway Station) **C2**
Sirkeci PTT Merkezi (Main Post Office) **B1**
SS Peter & Paul **B4**
Süleymaniye Hamamı **A2**
Witt Istanbul Suites **D5**
Yeni Camii (New Mosque) **B2**
Zülfaris Synagogue **C3**

Wander amid ancient **Byzantine and Ottoman *hans*** in a walk through the narrow streets of **Tahtakale**

Facing the Spice Market (*p.88*) on its western side is a part of Old Istanbul that still feels much as it must have done in its medieval heyday. Tahtakale ('Wooden Castle') is a warren of narrow streets, some too narrow for cars to pass, where locals still shop enthusiastically for everything from cheap packaging to hardware to freshly ground coffee. In the last couple of weeks of December it even fills up with 'Christmas' decorations, brought here now to celebrate the New Year.

Most of the shops are architecturally mundane, but interwoven among them are some extraordinarily ancient brick-built *hans*, where traders and their animals would once have been accommodated. Today, they are mainly used for storage.

Start looking for the *hans* around the base of the platform supporting the Rüstem Paşa Mosque, yet another beautiful work of Sinan. The oldest is the Balkapanı Han, which may date back to the 5th century, although the nearby Hurmalı Han (Date Han) is probably not much younger. Most colourful of all are the Büyük and Küçük Çukur Hans (Large and Small Sunken Hans) on the water-facing side of the mosque. In the narrow street between them you will still bump into aromatic stacks of spices waiting for customers as well as weary *hamals* (porters) taking a break between their onerous jobs.

Begin at Rüstem Paşa Mosque; map B2

Share a *simit* with the seagulls on a **ferry sailing from Eminönü**

Every morning, one of the iconic sights of Istanbul is the line-up of men selling *simits* – round bread rolls studded with sesame seeds – which are a local breakfast staple. These days, most make use of enclosed and licensed pushcarts, although you will still spot a few men striding about the place with trays piled high with interwoven *simits* as in the days of yore.

So much do Istanbullus like their *simits* that they even think that the seagulls deserve a share. It is quite routine for people to buy one extra *simit* to take with them on the ferries so that they can toss it to the squawking, greedy entourage of birds, many of them expert at snatching pieces of *simit* in mid-air.

The seagulls are an intrinsic part of the Istanbul experience whether you are listening to them crying from the rooftops or watching them flitting spectrally around the floodlit Blue Mosque. Not surprisingly, several of the city's most popular poets, including Yahya Kemal Beyaltı and Bedri Rahmi Eyüboğlu, celebrated the birds in their verse. But as you take that ferry ride with *simit* in hand, make sure to watch out for the Bosphorus' other resident birds – the cormorants that can always be seen spreading their wings in the sun or diving for fish, and the tiny Mediterranean shearwaters that skim the water in busy schools.

For ferry schedules from Eminönü to Üsküdar, Kadıköy and the Bosphorus, go to www.ido.com.tr; map C2

Give your senses a workout with **stuffed apricots and unusual Turkish cheeses** in the **Spice Market**

One of Istanbul's most atmospheric spots is the Spice Market, overlooking the waterfront at Eminönü and the New Mosque (*right*). The market was built in 1660, and its proceeds were used to fund the upkeep of the mosque. It was kept supplied by a caravan train from Egypt, hence its alternative name, the Egyptian Bazaar (Mısır Çarşısı). Although some of the hundred-odd shops beneath its vaulted ceilings now sell souvenirs, most still stick to a tried and tested formula of spices, herbs, flavoured teas and a great assortment of dried fruit and nuts, including delicious stuffed apricots and dates. Some also sell hefty wedges of rust-red *pastırma*, a garlic-flavoured pastrami particularly associated with the Central Anatolian city of Kayseri.

Don't leave without a look at the stalls that spill out on either side. On the western side, locals shop for regional cheeses, including a lovely soft sheep's milk cheese from Ezine, a herb-studded cheese from Van and a curious plaited cheese from Erzurum. On the eastern side, plants are sold alongside rather wretched animals. You can also buy a leech here for medicinal purposes...

Up a flight of stairs from the main entrance to the market (facing the New Mosque) is **Pandeli**, a dreamy turquoise-tiled dining room, with windows that look down on the bazaar below.

Spice Market (Mısır Çarşısı); Mon–Sat 10am–6pm; map B2
Pandeli; tel: 212-522 5534; www.pandeli. com.tr; Mon–Sat L only

Join the locals and **toss seeds to the pigeons** in front of the **New Mosque**

The New Mosque could only ever be described as 'new' in a city like Istanbul with a long and venerable history. In anyone else's book the fact that it was built between 1591 and 1633, at the behest of two of the more powerful female members of the Ottoman family – Safiye Sultan, the mother of Sultan Mehmed III, and Hatice Turhan Sultan, the mother of Sultan Mehmed IV – would make it pretty old.

The mosque has several noteworthy features including 66 domes, twin minarets with three balconies a piece to accommodate

half-a-dozen *muezzins* (the men who sing the call to prayer five times daily), and a wonderful, newly restored suite for the sultan, offering him private access to the mosque. You can spot the Royal Loge by looking up to the upper gallery on the left-hand side of the building.

Eminönü Meydanı, the piece of land immediately in front of the mosque, is Istanbul's equivalent of London's Trafalgar Square in the days before the pigeons were expelled. Here, you will find men and women selling trays of grain to be fed to the pigeons, which are revered in Islam. According to the ancient story, the Prophet Mohammed was in flight from his enemies and took refuge in a cave. A spider wove a web across the entrance and then a pigeon nested there, so it appeared as if no one could have entered recently and thus the prophet was saved. Many mosques now have areas set aside specifically for the feeding of pigeons.

The tomb of Hatice Turhan Sultan (daily 9.30am–4.30pm; free) is just opposite the mosque.

New Mosque (Yeni Camii); Eminönü Meydanı; daily, avoid prayer times; map B2

Admire **montages by the 'father of wall art'** at the **Istanbul Modern**

One of the warehouses attached to the port at Tophane on the Bosphorus has been turned into a light-filled art gallery. Since Islam's prohibition on images of living things only weakened comparatively recently, virtually all Turkish art is effectively modern art; almost everything here was painted in the 19th or 20th centuries. There is a fine collection of portraits, and some interesting landscapes that highlight just how much the city has changed over the last hundred years.

Names to conjure with include Şeker Ahmed Pasa, İbrahim Çallı, Hamit Görele and Fahrelnissa Zeid, but particularly interesting are the montages created by Istanbul-born, but New York-domiciled, Burhan Doğançay, an artist with a particular interest in walls and what people do to them

> **ISTANBUL BIENNIAL**
> For a two-month period (usually mid-Sept–mid-Nov) every odd year (eg 2011), contemporary art exhibitions crop up all over the city, with the Istanbul Modern providing the main venue. See www.iksv.org/bienal.

(www.burhandogancay.com). To find out more, visit the small **Doğançay Museum** in Balo Sokak off İstiklal Caddesi in Beyoğlu.

Istanbul Modern's basement hosts art and photography displays along with an art library and cinema. The gallery is also known for its excellent Turkish fusion **restaurant** (tel: 212-292 2612).

Istanbul Modern; Meclis-i Mebusan Caddesi, Tophane; tel: 212-234 7300; www.istanbulmodern.org; Tue–Sun 10am–6pm, Thur until 8pm; charge, free Thur; map E4

Hobnob with local students at the lively *nargile* cafés behind the Nusretiye Mosque

As the main road whizzes from the Galata Bridge across the Bosphorus towards Dolmabahçe, it passes through Tophane where, on the left-hand side of the road, you can see the multi-domed building that was once the city arsenal. Facing it across the road are the large Kılıç Ali Paşa Mosque complex, a work of Sinan, and the newly restored Tophane Fountain, one of the landmark fountains given to the city by the wealthy in the 18th century. Just up the road from the fountain is the Victory Mosque (Nusretiye Camii), given its name to celebrate Sultan Mahmud II's successful suppression of the ever-rebellious Janissary army in 1826 and its replacement with a modern standing army.

All these monuments are very conspicuous, but less so is the line-up of *nargile* (water-pipe) cafés tucked away behind the Nusretiye Mosque on the waterfront. Here you can lounge on a beanbag and join the backgammon players in a game while you puff on your pipe and try to imagine what the area would have looked like in the days when this was a military parade ground. Here, too, you can sample a *nargile* fired up with real tobacco rather than the ersatz flavoured varieties. *'Tömbeki'* tobacco is rough and strong. Try it at **Köşebaşı** (tel: 212-249 7936) if you dare.

Nargile cafés; head towards the water from beside the Nusretiye Mosque to find them; map D4

91

Grab a **fish sandwich** from the boats bobbing up and down at **Eminönü**

Another of the iconic sights of Istanbul is the line-up of fishermen always to be found on the Galata Bridge, their lines dangling over the side to catch an array of what always look like disappointingly small fry. On the Karaköy side of the bridge, the small, lively **Fish Market** (Balık Pazarı; map C3) retails what the fishing fleet brought in overnight: *levrek* (sea bass), *çıpura* (gilt-head bream) and *hamsi* (anchovies) – the latter a winter delicacy.

With so much fish on all sides, what could be better than to lunch on a fish sandwich, one of the cheap and cheerful snacks which make the Istanbul street-food scene such a pleasure? Fish sandwiches come as half loaves of bread, sliced in two and stuffed with a freshly grilled mackerel and a little bit of greenery. Until recently, they were sold in basic boats that moored perilously in between the Eminönü ferries (map C2). Now, however, they are served from rather more kitsch purpose-built floating kitchens by men dressed up in faux-Ottoman garb. No matter – they taste just as delicious.

While on the waterfront you could also push out the boat taste-wise and indulge in a plastic cupful of *turşu* (mixed pickles), an Istanbullu favourite. The pickle sellers also sell *şalgam*, the bitter turnip drink from Adana.

To eat fish in a more formal setting, head for **Kumkapı** (p.42) or the fish restaurants of the **Bosphorus** (p.169).

Treat yourself to some **rose-flavoured *lokum*** from the **original Turkish delight shop**

Turkish delight is as quintessentially Turkish as the huge red-and-white flags that festoon the city, and it started here in Sirkeci at the small shop of Ali Muhiddin Hacı Bekir. Born in the Black Sea province of Kastamonu, Bekir Efendi moved to Istanbul to start a confectionery shop in 1777, making this one of the oldest businesses in the city and perhaps the only one still using the same premises. He acquired the honorific 'Hacı' after making the pilgrimage to Mecca and went on to become chief confectioner to the sultan. We know what he looked like thanks to a watercolour drawn by the Maltese artist Amadeo Preziosi (1816–82) who depicted him as a burly, bearded man in a turban weighing up his *lokum* for a discreetly veiled female client.

Lokum, as the Turks call Turkish delight, is a chewy sweet, the production of which was facilitated by the introduction of cone-shaped blocks of sugar from Europe. In the early 19th century, the Germans started producing a starch that could be used instead of flour to thicken sweets. Shortly afterwards, a *lokum*-struck British tourist took some to England where it acquired its familiar nickname.

Rosewater flavouring was a big-time Ottoman favourite, so help yourself to some *gül lokumu* (rose *lokum*) to get in the mood.

Ali Muhiddin Hacı Bekir; Hamidiye Caddesi 83; tel: 212-522 0666; www. hacibekir.com.tr; map C2

Check out the **Orient Express silverware** in the **Sirkeci Station Museum**

When it first steamed into Sirkeci Station in 1888, the Orient Express was a wonder to behold. It was kitted out with every conceivable luxury to serve its upmarket clientele, who on arrival were conveyed by sedan chair to the Pera Palas Hotel *(p.105)*, built especially to host them on a hillside overlooking the Golden Horn. Not surprisingly, the train was immortalised in many novels, most famously in Agatha Christie's *Murder on the Orient Express* but also in Graham Greene's *Stamboul Express*. Unfortunately, all good things come to an end, and by 1977 when the service was finally decommissioned it was but a pale imitation of its former self.

Today, many visitors use Sirkeci Station without even noticing the lovely Oriental-Gothic facade designed in 1887 by the German architect August Jasmund (stained-glass window *pictured*), which was sidelined when a more modern entrance was tacked onto what was originally the side of the building. Even fewer visitors pause to visit the small museum inside the station, which contains a collection of relics rescued from the Orient Express, including some silverware fine enough to have graced a luxury hotel.

You can still dine like the original passengers in the station's Orient Express restaurant. Afterwards, you can also watch the whirling dervishes *(p.103)* in the old station events room (Fri and Sun, 7.30pm).

Orient Express Restaurant, Sirkeci Station, Istasyon Caddesi; tel: 212-522 2280; daily L and D; museum Tue-Sat 9am–5pm; free; map C2

Send your postcards from the magnificent **Main Post Office**, Turkish First National Architecture writ large

There may be a handy booth for postcards right in Sultanahmet Square, but you would be much better advised to take a short walk down to Sirkeci to do your mailing in the magnificent building created there between 1905 and 1909 by Vedat Tek. Along with Kemalettin Bey (the man who features on the reverse of the TL20 banknote), he was responsible for popularising what is now called the Turkish First National school of architecture, an attempt to express in stone the newly emerging sense of Turkish nationalism.

The post office has the same sort of grandeur as Victorian civic wonders such as Manchester Town Hall in England, and you can't help but feel that the actual postal functions are somewhat lost in the yawning internal space. But externally there are many admirable features: the little corner turrets, the panels of Kütahya tiles, the calligraphy on the facade. The small museum on one side even makes it possible to admire the lovely marble staircases as well as a large collection of ancient mailboxes and Turkish stamps.

Kemalettin Bey's work tended to place less emphasis

on decoration. There's a fine example nearby in what was once the First Vakıf Han (an early business centre) and is now the Legacy Ottoman Hotel (tel: 212-526-6767).

Main Post Office (Sirkeci PTT Merkezi); Büyük Posthane Caddesi; museum Mon–Fri 9am–5pm; free; map B1

Discover the **Gothic Arab Mosque**, a reminder of forgotten Genoese Istanbul, in **Karaköy**

To this day, Karaköy remains a grungily authentic neighbourhood, its backstreets packed with hardware shops and small restaurants catering to local workers – the sort of places where the action is over for the day by 3.30pm. Hard though it is to believe it now, this was

one a separate walled enclave extending along the waterfront and up as far as Galata Tower, which was self-governed by Istanbul's medieval Genoese trading community.

There's not much left to show for the Genoese today, but if you venture into the backstreets you will eventually stumble across the Arab Mosque, a huge building with a square bell tower unlike anything else in the city. Originally a church, the building served the Genoese community from 1337 until the early 16th century when it was converted into a mosque for the Moors who had been expelled from Spain in 1492.

With your appetite whetted for all things Genoese, you might want to track down the battered building in Kart Çınar Sokağı that started life as the *podesta*, or Genoese council. There is also a small stretch of wall here that dates back to Genoese times. The single most striking reminder of the Genoese is, however, the Galata Tower high up on the hill above Karaköy (*p.102*).

Arab Mosque (Arap Camii); Galata Mahkemesi Caddesi; daily but avoid prayer times; map B4

Watch a glorious **sunset over the Golden Horn** from beneath the **Galata Bridge**

So impressive is the Istanbul skyline that you can admire it at any time of day. Still, there's always something special about watching the sun go down over water, and Eminönü boasts a perfect place to soak up the sunset, namely the row of restaurants built along the lower deck of the Galata Bridge. Despite their somewhat garish neon-lit modern incarnation, these restaurants have a venerable history since the early 20th-century Galata Bridge, which survived until 1994, was well known for the ramshackle fish restaurants that clung to its underside.

It is a shame that the sun doesn't set on the side of the bridge that overlooks the historic buildings of Topkapı Palace, Hagia Sophia and the Blue Mosque. On the other hand, from the sunset side of the bridge you can gaze up towards the great Süleymaniye Mosque as it rides the summit of Istanbul's third hill and then across at the dramatic Galata Tower looming above the triple-windowed white building that once housed the Ottoman Bank. Immediately ahead of you will be the busy Atatürk Bridge, built in 1940.

A lot of sundowners are consumed beneath the bridge. The restaurants are nothing fancy – your choice may well come down to a toss-up between those that sell alcohol and those that don't.

Galata Bridge (Galata Köprüsü); map B3

97

Beyoğlu

Beyoğlu

0 100 200 300 400 500 m

0 100 200 300 400 500 yds

Inset map (See left):

General

House Café
Yazıcı Sk.
Refik
formerly Markiz Pastanesi
Müeyyet Sk.
Sofyalı 9
Gepici Sk.
Lokal
Casa Botter
İstiklal Cad.
KV Café
TÜNEL
Tünel Meydanı
Librairie de Pera
BEYOĞLU
Galata Mevlevihane
Belediye Cad.
Tramvay Sk.
Nergiz Sk.
Mesrutiyet Cad.
Müellif Cad.

Main map:

Tavla Sk.
Sakızağacı Sk.
Eski
Doğançay Müzesi
Tarlabaşı
Bulvarı
Abanoz Sk.
Balo
Büyük Bayram
Kamer Hatun Camii
Arslan Sk.
Hamalbaşı
Cumhuriyet Meyhane
Nevizade Sk.
Ney'le Mey'le
Emek Bayram
Avrupa Pasajı
Krependeki İmroz
İstiklal
Atlas
Ghetto
Halep Pasajı
Çiçek Pasajı
Balık Pazarı
Konak
Galata
Meşrutiyet Cad.
Hazzopulo Pasajı
Yapı Kredi Gallery
GALATASARAY
Büyük Londra
Mısır Apartmanı
Galatasaray Lisesi (Galatasaray Lycee)
Tarlabaşı
Çok Çok Thai
Kallavi Sk.
Yeni Çarşı
Üsküdar Bayr.
Taşkışla Sk.
Mezarlık Sk.
Mikla
Pera Müzesi (Pera Museum)
San Antoine Kilisesi (St Anthony)
Nuri Ziya Sk.
Hayriye Cad.
Retromc
TEPEBAŞI PARKI
ODAKULE
Pera Palas Oteli (Pera Palace Hotel)
Balyoz Sk.
Posta-cılar Sk.
Tomtom Kaptan Camii
ÇUKURC
Ansen Suites
Paşabahçe
Asmalımescit Sk.
Tomtom Kaptan Sk.
Bostanbaşı Cad.
Çukurcuma Cad.
Boğazkesen Cad.
Babylon
Santa Maria Draperis
H.
Cu
Richmond
İstiklal Cad.
Bostan İçerisi Çık.
See left
TÜNEL
Casa Botter
Leb-i Derya
Camcı Fevzi Sk.
İçerisi Çık.
BEYOĞLU
Galata Mevlevihane
Şah
Kumbaracı
İlk Belediye
To
Galip Dede Cad.
Crimean Church
TOPHAN
Beyoğlu Ticaret Lisesi
Yolcuzade İskender Cad.
Şişhane Sk.
N. Hanım Sk.
Büyük
Tulumba
Kılıç
Ps. Han
Yolcuzade Mekt. Sk.
Neve Shalom Synag.
Okçu Musa Cad.
Hendek Cad.
Serdar-ı Ekrem
Galata Kulesi (Galata Tower)
Yüksek Kaldırım Cad.
Türk
Sümak Sk.
Harput Sk.
Şair Ziya Paşa Cad.
Anemon Galata
Istanbul Holiday Apartments
Turkish Orth Patriarch
Azapkapı Çeşmesi
Yolcuzade
Yanıkkapı
Fırıldak Sk.
SS Peter & Paul
Berehetzade Camii
St. Benoit
Azapkapı Sokullu M. Paşa Camii
Arap Camii
Galata Mahkemesi
Voyvoda Cad.
Kemeraltı
Kasa Galeri
PERŞEMBE PAZARI PARKI
Tersane Cad.
Zincirli
Osmanlı Bankası Müzesi
KARAKÖY
Karaköy Meydanı
KARAKÖY

100

Scan a **360-degree panorama of the city** from the balcony of the **Galata Tower**

One of the most distinctive landmarks of the Beyoğlu skyline is the cylindrical Galata Tower with its witch's-hat roof. It has been standing here since 1349 when, as the Tower of Christ, it formed part of the walls surrounding the self-governing Genoese trading colony *(p.96)*.

Today, the tower is used as the venue for rather cheesy Turkish night-time entertainment, but during the day it provides one of the best vantage points from which to size up the city. Come here to get your bearings, and perhaps ponder the fact that this view enabled fire-watchers to look out for flames amid the city's wooden houses.

Of course, such a prominent monument has to have garnered its repertoire of stories, tall or otherwise. One such tale was related by the 17th-century Ottoman travel writer Evliya Çelebi, who reported that in 1638 a certain Hezarfen Ahmed Çelebi strapped on primitive wings and flew across from the tower to Üsküdar, thereby inaugurating the era of intercontinental flight. For his pains he was sent into exile by the sultan.

Until recently very down at heel, today the area around the tower has become extremely trendy. It is well worth exploring the narrow streets winding downhill behind it for the many cool boutiques and arty coffee shops.

Galata Tower (Galata Külesi); Galata Meydanı, Karaköy; tel: 212-293 8180; www.galatattower.net/english; daily 9am–8pm; charge; map C2

Arrive early for the best view of the **whirling dervish** *sema* in the **Galata Dervish Lodge**

Way back in the 13th century, Celaleddin Rumi, better known to the world as Mevlana, established a dervish order that became known for the tradition of whirling as a way of attaining mystical union with Allah. The whirling dervishes were a phenomenon that spread throughout the Ottoman Empire, but in 1925 they were disbanded by Atatürk as part of his effort to secularise Turkish society. In 1988 the dervishes were quietly allowed to resume their rituals. Now you can hardly move in the city for whirling dervishes, not all of them, it must be said, authentic mystics.

The Galata Dervish Lodge near Tünel is probably the most atmospheric place to see the dervishes in action. Newly restored, the lodge dates back to 1492, although the *semahane* (ritual room) in which you will watch the dervishes is a graceful 18th-century octagonal building. What makes watching the dervishes here such a pleasure is their proximity, especially if you arrive early to bag the best seats at the front. From here, you will be able to feel the whoosh of the undulating white robes worn by the dervishes and hear the swish of their feet passing over the wooden floor. The *sema* is preceded by a recital of dervish music, so expect to spend about two hours.

Galata Dervish Lodge (Galata Mevlevihane); Galipdede Caddesi 15, Tünel; tel: 212-245 4141; Wed-Mon 9.30am-5pm, check board outside for times of semas; charge; map C2

TÜNEL FUNICULAR

If you don't fancy the haul up the hill from the Galata Bridge to Tünel, then hop aboard the funicular on Tersane Caddesi (map C1) and ascend in style. Built in 1875, it is the second-oldest underground train in the world (after the London Underground), and it meets up in Tünel Square with another antique form of transport, the 19th-century İstiklal Caddesi tram *(p.106)*.

Train your eyes on *The Tortoise Trainer* by Osman Hamdi Bey in the **Pera Museum**

Sometimes an image can become almost too popular for its own good, and that's the fate that has befallen *The Tortoise Trainer*, the masterpiece of the Turkish orientalist artist, archaeologist and museum-creator Osman Hamdi Bey (1842–1910). Ever since it sold at auction in 2004 for a record-breaking sum of money, crude reproductions of the picture – which depicts a dervish training tortoises that would carry candles on their backs in the Topkapı Palace garden – have cropped up all over town. Fortunately, the original is big and impressive enough to stand up to all the hype.

Pera Museum is a state-of-the-art private gallery containing an impressive collection of landscape images of Istanbul. The work of Osman Hamdi Bey aside, you may want to look out in particular for pictures by the late 19th-century court painter Fausto Zonaro and by the Maltese artist Amadeo Preziosi.

Elsewhere in the museum, there is a collection of pottery from Kütahya, the town that succeeded İznik as the centre of the ceramics industry, and another of ancient Anatolian weights and measures. On the ground floor the fine café has a whiff of *fin-de-siècle* Vienna about it. The museum shop is one of the best in Turkey.

Pera Museum (Pera Müzesi); Meşrutiyet Caddesi 65, Tepebaşı; tel: 212-334 9900; www.peramuzesi.org.tr; Tue–Sat 9am–6pm, Sun noon–6pm; charge; map C3

Say cheers to Agatha Christie with a **gin and tonic** at the bar of the period-piece **Pera Palas Hotel**

Overlooking the Golden Horn in trendy Tepebaşı stands the Pera Palas, a hotel forever associated with the Orient Express *(p.94)* for the passengers of which it was purpose-built by the Levantine architect Alexandre Vallaury in 1892. The Pera Palas is one of those extraordinary hotels which everybody who is anybody seems to have graced with their presence, among them the actress Greta Garbo, President Tito of ex-Yugoslavia, King Edward VIII, and a trio of spies – Mata Hari, Kim Philby and Cicero. But probably the most famous guest of all was the novelist Agatha Christie, who put up here in 1934 while she was writing what became one of her best-known books, *Murder on the Orient Express*. Christie stayed in room 411, which was once believed to contain a key that would help explain where she was during her mysterious 11-day disappearance in December 1926. Needless to say, it didn't.

Newly restored, the Pera Palas sports the thoroughly congenial Orient Bar, as well as an exquisite ground-floor cake shop. Original features include the lift that used to whisk guests up to their rooms. One of them would have been Mustafa Kemal Atatürk, the first president of Turkey, who liked to stay in room 101, now preserved as a museum.

Pera Palas Hotel; Meşrutiyet Caddesi 52; tel: 212-222 8090; www.perapalace. com; map C3; see also p.172

See bustling **İstiklal Caddesi** from a **nostalgic tram**, then stroll back along it admiring the monuments

The street in Istanbul where you can really take the pulse of the modern city is İstiklal Caddesi (İstiklal or 'Independence' Street), the busy pedestrian thoroughfare that wends its way south from Taksim Square (map E5) to Tünel and Galata. No matter what time of day, you are guaranteed to find it thronged with window-shoppers, cinema-goers, bar-hoppers, would-be diners and just plain passers-by, catered to by a fast-changing line-up of shops and restaurants.

The best – if not the speediest – way to get from one end of the street to the other is to hop aboard the cute little red-and-white tram that makes its way up and down

it three times an hour with small boys clinging to its sides. A reminder of the many trams that once served the city, it first came into service in 1875. Today, the tram is a city symbol, at its most picturesque on holidays when adorned with jaunty red flags.

It is well worth walking back along İstiklal Caddesi to inspect the monuments left over from the days when, as the Grande Rue de Pera, this was the heart of European Istanbul, home to most of the embassies and churches. In Taksim Square you can admire the surprisingly small monument to the creation of the Turkish Republic in 1923, before striking off

down the street. Immediately on the left loom the dome and towers of Hagia Triada (Holy Trinity), the huge Greek Orthodox church built in 1880 after the repeal of a law forbidding church domes. Right on İstiklal, the French Consulate was originally built as a plague hospital in the 18th century.

Further along on the right is the Ağa Camii (1594), the street's only mosque. Past the Flower Arcade (*p.109*) and Fish Market (*p.108*) on the right, across the road you will see the gates of the Galatasaray High School, once attended by the city's rich and famous.

At this point İstiklal crosses Yeni Çarşı Sokak. The junction is marked by a memorial to the 50th anniversary of the Republic, while on the far side stands the Yapı Kredi Gallery, home to many excellent free exhibitions. Keep heading south and you will pass on the left the arch leading to the cathedral of St Anthony (*below*). A bit further on and steps on the left lead down to the colourful barrel-vaulted church of Santa Maria Draperis built in 1904.

Once upon a time you could have stopped for tea on the right in the lovely Markiz Pastanesi (Patisserie), with its impressive Art Nouveau tiles, but this is now a fast-food joint. Across the road is the crumbling Casa Botter, an Art Nouveau extravaganza designed by the Italian architect Raimondo d'Aronco in 1901. The walk finishes at the Tünel (map C2).

ST ANTHONY'S CATHEDRAL

In the days when İstiklal Caddesi was the hub of the city's European society, St Anthony's (map C4) was just one of the many churches to be found in and immediately off the street. Built between 1906 and 1911 by Guilio Mongeri, it is a hybrid of Italian architecture on the outside and French neo-Gothic on the inside. Like many of the churches here it still offers services on Sundays (in English 10am; weekdays 8am) and Christian holidays.

Brave a new taste sensation with **fried mussels or a** *kokoreç* **sandwich** in the historic **Fish Market**

Midway along İstiklal Caddesi, facing southwest, you will see the Flower Arcade (Çiçek Pasajı) on the right with the Fish Market (Balık Pazarı) running by it. Once the best place in the city to buy fresh fish, this arcade is now better known for its fruit and vegetable stalls and tiny delicatessens, as well as for the Avrupa Pasajı jutting out on one side and an inviting place to shop for souvenirs.

As you start down the alley, you will quickly come to a cluster of small cafés selling popular Turkish snacks, including deep-fried mussels that are served on skewers to eat in or take away. Here, too, you'll come across

kokoreç, a meaty delicacy that most non-Turks approach with trepidation since it consists of lamb entrails roasted on a grill, then sliced up and stuffed inside a half-loaf of bread. Doesn't sound so lip-smackingly tempting? Never fear – it tastes just great.

The Fish Market is not the only place to try out new taste sensations. Wander back out onto İstiklal and you will soon bump into a street vendor selling mussels stuffed with rice mixed with pine kernels and currants, or men retailing roasted chestnuts, a firm favourite with the late-night set.

Fish Market (Balık Pazarı); map D4

Pass your time in 19th-century style in İstiklal Caddesi's **hidden shopping arcades**

In the 19th century what was then Pera and is now Beyoğlu was home to most of the city's European residents. Over in Old Istanbul many locals still shopped in *hans* and bazaars but in Pera they preferred arcades like those of Paris and London, most of them opening off İstiklal Caddesi, then the Grande Rue de Pera. The most famous such arcade (called a *pasaj* in Turkish) was – and is – the Çiçek Pasajı (Flower Arcade), which is crammed full of *meyhanes* (taverns), but several other survivors are also well worth scouting out.

Heading down İstiklal Caddesi from Taksim Square, you come first to the Rumeli Pasajı, with an elaborate facade that incorporates its name in Latin, Greek and Arabic, testament to the multicultural nature of the 19th-century city. Upstairs in the Emek Pasajı, the **Yeşilcam Café** is decorated with mid-20th-century film posters from the days when this part of town was 'Yeşilcam', Turkey's Little Hollywood.

Further down the road, the Halep Pasajı (Aleppo Arcade) contains a theatre and cinema as well as shops selling replica Anatolian amulets and alternative paraphernalia. Facing it, the more elegant Atlas Pasajı is chock-full of designer bags and T-shirts.

The most Bond Street of all the arcades is the Avrupa Pasajı (European Arcade; *pictured*), which opens off the Fish Market (*left*). Festooned with neoclassical statuettes, it's a great place to browse for old posters, postcards and the odd vinyl album.

On the far side of Yeni Çarşı Caddesi watch for the cast-iron Art Nouveau facade of Aznavur Pasajı. Close by is the Hazzopulo Pasajı where a shop-filled passage opens out into a cobbled courtyard hosting İstiklal Caddesi's last traditional tea garden.

Yeşilcam Café; Emek Pasajı, İstiklal Caddesi 122/1; tel: 212-293 7279; daily B, L and D; map D4

Sip **tea with the locals** beneath shady trees at the **Firuz Ağa Mosque**

İstiklal Caddesi is the best known of the streets fanning out from Taksim Square, but it's also worth walking down almost equally busy Sıraselviler (Row of Cypresses) Caddesi, heart of the popular residential district called Cihangir in memory of one Sultan Süleyman the Magnificent's sons. The top (Taksim) end of the street is well known for its nightlife and for a cluster of hotels, but if you keep walking downhill you will eventually come to a road junction dominated by a mosque, painted green; its signs indicate that it dates back to 1491, although the current incarnation was only erected in 1823. Facing the main road to one side is **Firuz**, a shady tea garden (actually several merged into one) which is a popular local meeting place.

Many people still associate Turkey with coffee, but today tea (*çay*) is actually the drink that keeps the wheels of life turning. Here, though, tea is drunk in a way that will be unfamiliar to most foreign visitors. It would be anathema to a Turk to add milk to their tea or to slosh it into a mug. Instead, it is always served in a small tulip-shaped glass, with copious quantities of sugar obligatory. The tea, much of it grown on the Black Sea, is served from a double-burner, diluted to taste. Newcomers often find it too strong – ask for it *'açık'* (light) for a more palatable experience. Apple tea (*elma çay*) is a wholly chemical alternative offered to tourists; *oralet* is an equally chemical orange tea that also finds favour with the locals.

Want to buy your own Turkish tea glasses? Try **Paşabahçe** on İstaklal Caddesi (150).

Firuz Café; Sıraselviler Caddesi; tel: 212-252 0241; map E3

Scout out a bargain in the **antiques and textiles shops of Çukurcuma**

Tucked in a dip between İstiklal Caddesi and Sıraselviler Caddesi, Çukurcuma is a trendy area full of cute little one-off antique shops, boutiques and cafés, the antithesis of increasingly homogenised İstiklal Caddesi. Come here to pick your way through piles of old embroidery recovered from grandma's dowry box or to choose a chair to be reupholstered. Some of the shops have been here forever and their owners know the precise value of every last button. Others are johnny-come-latelies, where you may still be able to pick up a bargain.

Some of the Çukurcuma shops are just for window-shopping, others for parting with serious cash. At **Tombuk** (Çukurcuma Camii Sokak 7) you can ponder the sheer number of items that used to be made from marble, while at **Leyla** (Altı Patlar Sokağı 6A) you can rifle through piles of embroidery. **Üsküdarlı Bayram** (Faikpaşa Caddesi 26A) is instantly recognisable by the London Transport request bus stop sign standing outside; it sells everything from bric-a-brac to valuable antiques. **Kuti Retromodern** (Faikpaşa Caddesi 51A) shows off all sorts of snazzy lighting, while **Roman** (Ağa Hamam Sokak 34) reworks everything from old milk churns to battered chairs to give them new life.

Çukurcuma; map D3

Down a *raki* with mezes and fish at a *meyhane* on boisterous **Nevizade Sokak**

One unexpected relic of Beyoğlu's past cosmospolitanism is the number of *meyhanes* (taverns) that survive here. Once heavy drinking dens where the food was almost incidental to the alcohol and music, most are now much more female-friendly places with lengthy unwritten menus to choose from.

The most famous gathering of *meyhanes* can be found inside the cobbled courtyard of the Flower Arcade (Çiçek Pasajı), which was named after the White Russian flower-sellers who used to haunt it. Today, however, the liveliest action has migrated to Nevizade Sokak, the street behind it, where on a summer night you will have trouble finding a table despite the number of restaurants.

Grab a seat, make yourself comfortable and prepare to enjoy yourself. Waiters will bring a tray of mezes (appetisers) for you to choose from. What with the beans, the cheeses, the calamari, the *böreks* (pastries) and the assorted dips, you may never get as far as the fish or grilled meats that serve as main courses, let alone the fruit that comes as dessert. All this should be washed down with quantities of *raki*, or 'lion's milk', the aniseed-flavoured liquor that is a Turkish favourite; but no one will quibble if you stick with wine or beer. Musicians will pass around the tables, as will street vendors offering fresh almonds on ice for those with space to spare. No one ever leaves Nevizade disappointed.

As for which *meyhanes* on Nevizade Sokak to try, there's the long-lived **Krependeki İmroz Restaurant**; (24; tel: 212-249 9073; map D4) and the more upstart **Ney'le Mey'le** (12; tel: 212-249 9073; map D4). At the Fish Market around the corner, there's **Cumhuriyet Meyhanesi** (Sahne Sokak 47; tel: 212-243 6406; map C4), with enough testimonials on its walls to keep you reading all night.

See and be seen with the in crowd at a fashionable rooftop bar and restaurant

What makes for a great night out in Istanbul? Well, here as elsewhere you will be wanting to find somewhere where the food and drink are guaranteed to be top-notch. But in Istanbul the view is really the thing, so the most happening places in Beyoğlu also tend to be those that scoop the best views – and that almost always means that they are up high.

Not surprisingly, **360** boasts an all but 360-degree panorama of the city (pictured) from its perch on top of the grand Mısır Apartımanı building on İstiklal Caddesi. Here the chefs whip up a grand selection of trendy fusion dishes which perfectly complement the views.

At **Mikla** on the roof of the Marmara Pera hotel a signature dish is *hamsi* (anchovies) on crispy toast, taking a traditional Turkish favourite and giving it a 21st-century twist.

Leb-i Derya ('Lip of the Sea') runs with a similar fusion recipe to 360. It has a second branch on the top floor of the Richmond Hotel (p.176) on İstiklal Caddesi.

Don't expect to get a table at any of these restaurants without a reservation, especially at weekends. And don't forget to don your glad rags – these are places where dressing to kill is almost as important as the food.

360; Mısır Apartımanı, İstiklal Caddesi 311/32; tel: 212-244 8192; www.360istanbul.com; map C4
Mikla; Meşrutiyet Caddesi 117; tel: 212-293 5656; www.miklarestaurant.com; map C3
Leb-i Derya; Kumbaracı Yokuşu 115/7; tel: 212-293 4989; www.lebiderya.com; map C2

Stumble upon an unexpected piece of Little Britain at the **Crimean Memorial Church**

Just downhill from the Tünel end of İstiklal Caddesi, visitors are often surprised to come across a piece of High Victorian Gothic architecture amid the mix of fine 19th-century mansion blocks and shoddy 21st-century concrete high-rises. The Crimean Memorial Church is exactly what its name suggests – a memorial to those who fell during the Crimean War of 1853–6 that pitched Britain and the Ottoman Empire against Russia. It was designed by George Edmund Street, the man responsible for the phantasmagoric Royal Courts of Justice building on the Strand in London. Street had come second to William Burges of Cardiff Castle fame in a competition to design the church, only to have the job fall into his lap when time actually came to begin work. Strangely enough, he designed the whole thing from afar, never setting foot in Istanbul even to admire the completed venture.

Despite being set in a garden oasis, the stone-built Crimean Church might seem rather austere were it not for the colourful panels adorning the organ loft which were painted by a Levantine artist, and the even more extraordinary panels on the rood screen. These were designed

by the Scottish artist Mungo McCosh and incorporate not just a backdrop of the Istanbul skyline but also icons of local life; look closely and you'll see that the Christ Child is clasping a *simit*. Even more intriguingly, the faces of the saints are those of expat and local luminaries, among them journalists and the Greek Patriarch, whose face is imposed on that of St John Chrysostom, his very distant predecessor.

Crimean Memorial Church; Anglican services on Sundays at 10am; map C2

Acquire a nose for the rich variety of **Turkish wine** at the **Kayra Academy**

Chances are, you won't know much about Turkish wine, which until recently boasted an unenviable reputation for inconsistency. Nowadays, however, a growing number of boutique wineries are bringing quality and confidence to the industry. To find out what's what, start by signing up for a course at the **Kayra Academy**, which provides tuition for everyone from complete novices through to would-be sommeliers. At least seven participants are required for a beginner's class, which takes place on the fourth floor of a 19th-century mansion block that also houses a wine-lovers' library and a super-stylish restaurant.

Once you've got your nose in, you can shop for a range of wines at the wonderful **La Cave** (Sıraselviler Caddesi 109, Cihangir; www.lacavesarap. com; map E3), downhill from the Kayra Academy on Sıraselviler Caddesi. Snap up a bottle of Sauvignon Blanc from Côte d'Avanos, a 900 Fume Blanc from Sevilen, an Isinda from Lykia Wineries, a Boğazkere from Urla Winery, a Centum from Sevilen or a Cabernet Reserve from Büyülübağ and you are unlikely to go home disappointed.

No time for studying or shopping? Then head straight for **Rouge** (Lamartin Caddesi, Talimhane; tel: 212-237 0190), a wine bar in trendy Talimhane, across the road from Taksim Square. It stocks 150 different labels and sells 50 different wines by the glass.

Kayra Akademi; Sıraselviler Caddesi 55, Cihangir; tel: 212-252 9161; www. kayraakademi.com; map E4

Bop till you drop to world-class sounds at the **Babylon nightclub**

Turkey may be a largely Muslim country, but it is also one with a youthful population that knows how to enjoy itself and rates good music. Athough there are large-scale concert halls scattered about the city, Beyoğlu has long held the monopoly on smaller-scale and more intimate venues. One of the best is **Babylon**, off fashionable Asmalımescit, which boasts a world-class sound system and has hosted such acts as the Turkish jazz musician Mercan Dede, the punk priestess Patti Smith and the crossover classical violin-player Nigel Kennedy. Concert over, you can wander into any number of trendy restaurants that stay open really late in summer.

Other popular venues within walking distance of Babylon include the somewhat grungier

Roxy (Aslan Yatağı Sokak 7; tel: 212-249 1283; map E4) and **Ghetto** (Kamer Hatun Caddesi 10; tel: 212-251 750; map D4), a summer-only venue housed inside an ex-bakery.

For something earthier and more ad hoc, the narrow streets running off İstiklal Caddesi are home to myriad *türkü* bars where you can listen to Turkish folk music in its modern incarnation. Wailing clarinets, beating drums – you'll be dancing before you've had time to think about it. Good streets to investigate include Zambak Sokak, Bekar Sokak, Mis Sokak, Büyükparmakkapı Sokak and Balo Sokak.

Babylon; Şeyhbender Sokak 3, Asmalımescit; tel: 212-292 7368; www.babylon-ist.com, other tickets from www.biletix.com; map C3

Round off the day with a **nightcap** beneath the twinkling lights of the **KV Café**

Not so long ago it was the Taksim end of İstiklal Caddesi that grabbed all the attention. These days, however, much of the buzz, certainly with the gourmet set, has migrated to the Tünel end of the street and particularly to the neighbourhood called Asmalımescit which runs parallel with İstiklal on the Golden Horn side. To find it, come out at the top end of the Tünel funicular (*p.103*) and walk straight ahead into Tünel Geçidi, an almost absurdly pretty arcade of which the far end opens into Asmalımescit.

Tünel Geçidi is lined with antiques shops and restaurants, alluring at any time of day. Come here in the evening, however, and you will find fairy lights threaded through the bushes, making it an absolutely magical place in which to dine or just stop off for a late-night coffee ('KV' is a play on *kahve*, the Turkish word both for coffee and for a place to drink it).

In summer Asmalımescit is so popular that you will struggle to find a seat at any of the myriad pavement restaurants without a reservation. Other than KV, good places to try include **The House Café** (Sümbül Sokak

9/1–2; tel: 212-351 4716), a handy branch of a chain restaurant that brought such Middle Eastern treats as falafels to Istanbul menus; **Sofyalı 9** (9; tel: 212-245 0362) and **Refik** (7; tel: 212-245 7879), two fish and meze hang-outs on Sofyalı Sokak; and the **Lokal** (Müeyyet Sokak 9; tel: 212-245 5743), a cosy Asian fusion cookery joint.

KV Café; Tünel Geçidi; tel: 212-251 4338; daily L and D; map B4

117

Beşiktaş and Dolmabahçe

Beşiktaş and Dolmabahçe

0 100 200 300 400 500 m
0 100 200 300 400 500 yds

N

Yıldız Hamidiye Camii

Barbaros Bulvari

Barış Sk.

Ihlamur Yıldız Cad.

Posta Cad.

Yıldız Cd.

Nüzhetiye Cad.

Ihlamur Deresi Cad.

Uzunçova Cad.

Kebapçı İskender

Hüsrev Gerede Cad.

Şehit Mehmet Sk.

Dizi Sk.

Ihlamur Kasrı (Ihlamur Pavilions)

Mısırlı Cad.

Ihlamur Deresi Cad.

Mecidt Ali Sk.

Barbaros Bulvari

Yıldız Cd.

Conrad Otel

Kılıçoğlu Sk.

Posta Cad.

Şeyh Zafir Camii

Serencebey Yokuşu

Çittenbik

Eski Yıldız Cd.

Ali Bey Sk.

Hilton

Kadırgalar Cad.

Maçka Çeşmesi

MAÇKA

TAŞKIŞLA

ŞİŞLİ

Taşkışla Cad.

Silahhane Sk.

Maçka Cad.

Armağan Sk.

Spor Cad.

Eytam Cad.

Şair

Nedim

Oyuncabıye

Şehit Asım Cad.

Süleyman Seba Cad.

Sinan Pasa Köprü Sk.

Sinanpaşa Camii

Çırağan Cad.

MAÇKA PARKI

Bayıldım Cad.

Vişnezade Camii Önü Sk.

Enis Akaygen Sk.

Valide Çeşmesi

Spor Cad.

W Oteli

Dolmabahçe Cad.

Kaşıkçı Sk.

Istanbul Technical University

Baruthane

Kadırgalar Cad.

TAŞLIK PARKI

Bakla Eferdi Sk.

Visnezade Takke Sk.

Deniz Müzesi (Naval Museum)

Cezayir Cad.

İnönü Stadyumu

Gazhane Bostanı Sk.

Dolmabahçe Cad.

Swissôtel The Bosphorus

Çamlı Köşk

Resim ve Heykel Müzesi (Painting and Sculpture Museum)

Istanbul Technical University

Gümüşsuyu Askeri Hast.

Mühendislik Fakülteleri

Gazhanesi Cad.

Dolmabahçe Cad.

Dolmabahçe Sarayı (Dolmabahçe Palace)

TAKSİM PARKI

Mete Cad.

İnönü (Gümüşsuyu) Cad.

Atatürk Cultural Centre

Mithatpaşa Cad.

Gümüşsuyu Cad.

Beytül Sk.

Çifte Vav Sk.

Ağa Vırağı Sk.

Matbah

Haci İzzet Paşa Cad.

İnebolu Cad.

Mebusan Cad.

Dolmabahçe Saat Kulesi (Clocktower)

Dolmabahçe Camii

TAKSİM

Meclisi

Saray

Mebusan Cad.

Yokuşu

Nebacağı Yokuşu

Nesetbaşı

KABATAŞ

KABATAŞ VAPUR İSKELESİ

DENİZ OTOBÜSÜ İSKELESİ

Kabataş-Üsküdar (Araba Vapurları) (Ferry Boat)

Kabataş-Adalar-Yalova-Çınarcık

Fındıklı Molla Çelebi Camii

FINDIKLI PARKI

Necatibey Cad.

120

Banyan **G4**
Büyük Mecidiye Camii
　(Büyük Mecidiye Mosque) **G4**
Camlı Köşk **C2**
Çırağan Palace Kempinski **E3**
City and Yıldız Palace Museums **E5**
Conrad Hotel **D4**
Deniz Müzesi (Naval Museum) **D3**
Dolmabahçe Camii **B2**
Dolmabahçe Sarayı
　(Dolmabahçe Palace) **C2**
Fındıklı Parkı **A1**
Four Seasons Bosphorus **E3**
Hilton **A3**
Ihlamur Kasrı (Ihlamur Pavilions) **C4**

İnönü Stadyumu **B2**
Küçük Mecidiye Camii
　(Küçük Mecidiye Mosque) **E4**
Lavanta **G4**
Maçka Parkı **B3**
Malta Köşkü (Malta Pavilion) **E4**
Ortaköy Meydanı **G4**
Radisson Blu Bosphorus Hotel **F4**
Şale Köşkü (Chalet Pavilion) **E5**
Şeyh Zafir Camii **D4**
Swissôtel The Bosphorus **B3**
Taşlık Parkı **B3**
W Hotel **C3**
Yıldız Parkı **E4**
Zuma **F4**

Kabataş can be reached by tram from Sultanahmet
or by funicular from Taksim Square. Bus 25RE runs to Ortaköy.

Swoon over the graceful **caiques** in the **Naval Museum**

Day or night, the Bosphorus is always busy with boats, from the giant tankers that plough up and down between the Mediterranean and Black seas to the ferries and pleasure craft that cut across it from side to side. Today, you can cross from the European to the Asian side of the Bosphorus using two huge bridges, but in Ottoman times there were not even coastal roads and the only means of getting about the city was by boat.

As the gondolas are to Venice, so the caiques were to Old Istanbul – sleek, beautiful boats designed to get the wealthy about in style. The more important the individual, the bigger their caique and the more oarsmen required to row it. Most of these lovely boats have disappeared, but you can eye up some of the surviving imperial

> **ADMIRABLE ADMIRAL**
> In the square facing the museum look out for the memorial to Barbarossa (c.1478–1546), the greatest of all the Ottoman admirals, who is buried in the double-decker tomb on the far side.

caiques in the Naval Museum right beside the waterfront at Beşiktaş – the oldest was used to get Sultan Mehmed IV around Istanbul in the 17th century.

In summer you can cruise between the Dolmabahçe, Beylerbeyi and Küçüksu palaces in a replica caique operated by the Sultan's Boat company (tel: 212-268 0299).

Naval Museum (Deniz Müzesi); Beşiktaş Caddesi; tel: 212-261 0040; Tue–Sun 9am–5pm; charge; map D3

Feast on an unexpected **oriental supper** at the **Zuma Restaurant** in Ortaköy

Turkish cuisine may rank as one of the world's greatest, but one of the main complaints of long-stay visitors to the city from big multicultural cities like London and Paris used to be the dearth of places to eat anything but Turkish cuisine. But all that has started to change as the Turks wised up first to the joys of Italian food, then to Japanese and now to virtually anything else the world's chefs care to dish up.

One of the best of the new ethnic restaurants is Zuma, which sits right beside the water at Ortaköy in a light-filled box of a building with a garden in front of it for summer dining. Zuma already has branches in London and Hong Kong, where it serves a menu that features not just the familiar sushi and *robata* (and sake, of course) but also some local specialities; in Istanbul these specialities also include sardines and bluefish. Food is served informally in a style known as *izakaya* that encourages sharing. Located in an up-market part of town, right beside the Radisson Blu Bosphorus hotel, the Zuma is not a cheap place for a night out. If you need to keep an eye on the budget, try visiting at lunch time, when a set menu aimed at business travellers keeps the bill in check.

Where else to find Asian food in Istanbul? You could always try **Çok Çok Thai** in Tepebaşi (Meşrutiyet Caddesi 51, Beyoğlu; tel: 212-292 6496), or **Dubb** (İncili Çavuş Sokak; tel 212-513 7308), a decent Indian restaurant in Sultanahmet.

Zuma; Salhane Sokak 7, Ortaköy; tel: 212-236 2296; www.zumarestaurant. com; daily L and D; map F4

Escape the madding crowds at the sprawling palace complex in peaceful Yıldız Park

Despite covering some 50,000 sq m of prime real estate just across the road from the Çırağan Palace Hotel *(right)*, Yıldız Park is often overlooked by visitors. This is a shame since it is liberally dotted with monuments to the last years of the Ottoman Empire. It was in 1866 that Sultan Abdülhamid II had the Balyans family *(p.127)* rebuild the State Apartments here so that he could retreat inland from Dolmabahçe Palace, which he felt to be far too exposed to attack from the water. Unfortunately, the sultan was so paranoid that he even moved out of these apartments and took refuge in the Şale Köşkü (Chalet Pavilion; *pictured*), a large guesthouse that had been built in easy stages, mainly to accommodate Kaiser Wilhelm II on his two visits to Istanbul at the end of the 19th century.

The Şale is open to the public although the state apartments are not. Ditto the delightful private theatre built so that the sultan could indulge his taste for the theatrical without leaving the park. But it is also worth dropping in on the City and Yıldız Palace museums, side by side in the grounds; the latter containing examples of woodwork carved by the sultan himself.

The hilly park makes a great place for a walk on a summer evening. Make sure to stop for tea at the Malta Köşkü (Malta Pavilion), which has a lovely marble pool inside it.

Yıldız Park; Çırağan Caddesi; 9am–6pm; free; map E4, E5; Şale and City and Yıldız Palace museums; Tue–Wed and Fri–Sun, summer 9.30am–5pm, winter until 4pm; charge; map E5

Delight in a glorious **swim or afternoon tea** at the sumptuous **Çırağan Palace Kempinski Hotel**

These days, there are a growing number of hotels on the banks of the Bosphorus, especially on the European side. However, few can boast such an illustrious history as the Çırağan Palace, which was built by the Balyans for Sultan Abdülaziz on the site of a much older palace. The sultan moved in during 1874, only to move out again within days complaining of the damp. Abdülaziz died soon after in 1876 in circumstances that left it unclear whether he committed suicide or was murdered. He was succeeded by his nephew Murad V who was deposed after only 93 days in favour of Abdülhamid II, whereupon poor Murad was imprisoned in the Çırağan Palace. There he remained for the rest of his life in straitened circumstances that belie the palace's present incarnation as a super-luxury hotel.

Actually the palace burnt down in 1910, and what guests stay in now is a rebuilt version that opened in 1990. Not that anyone who has been here would quibble with its palatial quality. Drop into the glorious lounge for afternoon tea or buy a day pass to use the wonderful infinity swimming pool, which stretches out on the terrace until it reaches the edge of the Bosphorus, treating bathers to the illusion that they could actually swim out and join the cormorants busily fishing in the water.

Çırağan Palace Kempinski Hotel; Çırağan Caddesi 32; tel: 212-326 4646; swimming pool: 7am-11pm; €100 midweek, €160 weekend; afternoon tea: TL 65; map E3

Weigh up modern Turkish history beside **Atatürk's deathbed** in the **Dolmabahçe Palace**

If there is one figure who dominates modern Turkish history it has to be Mustafa Kemal Atatürk, the war hero who led the country from defeat in World War I to victory in the Turkish War of Independence (1919–22), and who went on to become the country's first president and the greatest reformer Turkey has ever known. As part of his programme of reforms, it was Atatürk who decided to move the capital away from Istanbul to Ankara in the heart of Anatolia, thereby cementing the break with the Ottoman past.

Ironically, although Atatürk is buried in the Anıtkabir monument in Ankara, he actually died in Dolmabahçe, the palace on the Bosphorus built by Abdülmecid, one of the later sultans, in an earlier attempt to modernise the crumbling empire. In October 1938 Atatürk had been dining on the state yacht, the *Savarona*, when he was taken ill. He was conveyed to the palace, where he died at 9.05am on 11

November. Since then, all the clocks in the palace have been frozen at that moment, which is also commemorated countrywide by a minute's silence on its anniversary every year.

A visit to the room in which Atatürk died, where the bed is draped with a Turkish flag, is one of the highlights of the rather rushed guided tours of the palace that are the only way of seeing it. You should first take a turn around the gardens so that you can savour the architecture, a complete break with the pretty kiosks and cloisters of the Topkapı Palace on the other side of the Bosphorus. The buildings were designed by Garabet and Nikoğos Balyan, members of a prolific family of Ottoman-Armenian architects whose handiwork is also on show in the Beylerbeyi and Küçüksu palaces on the Asian side of the city (p.164 and p.168). The Balyans favoured a lavish Rococo style of architecture that many modern visitors will find over the top. It is matched by a lavish style of interior decoration that mixes and matches Bohemian crystal, Yıldız porcelain, mother-of-pearl inlay and enormous oriental carpets to somewhat overpowering effect.

Atatürk's apartment aside, the most impressive single room in the palace is the Memorial Hall, which traditionally divided the public male part of the building (the Selamlık) from the private family areas (the Harem). With a concealed dome supported by 56 columns, it is said to be the largest throne room in the world; just installing the giant chandelier took some three months. It was here that Atatürk gave his first speech as the president of the new Republic.

CAMLI KÖŞK

If the palace itself can seem a little overwhelming, you should find time to visit the cute Camlı Köşk (Glass Pavilion) attached to the exterior wall. Just as exuberantly decorated with crystal piano legs and paintings of demure-looking big cats lining the ceiling, it has been beautifully restored and has a very appealing cohesiveness.

Dolmabahçe Palace (Dolmabahçe Sarayı); Dolmabahçe Caddesi, Beşiktaş; Tue–Wed and Fri–Sun, summer 9am–4pm, winter 9am–3pm, separate guided tours of Selamlık and Harem – if short of time, skip the Harem; map C2

Discover forgotten **Turkish Art Nouveau** at the unique **Şeyh Zafır Mosque**

When most people think about Turkish architecture they home in immediately on the great Ottoman architect Sinan and his gifts to the city in the form of such masterpieces as the Süleymaniye, Rüstem Paşa and Sokullu Mehmed Paşa mosques. But towards the end of the 19th century, at the very time when the Ottoman Empire was falling apart, several European architects also made a mark on the city.

One of them was Italian-born Raimondo d'Aronco (1857–1932), the genius behind the unique Şeyh Zafır Mosque, tucked away in a Beşiktaş side street very close to the Conrad Hotel (p.173).

Şeyh Zafır was a dervish and a spiritual adviser to the troubled Sultan Abdülhamid II who spent most of his reign hiding away from his subjects in Yıldız Palace. D'Aronco had come to Istanbul in 1893 to design buildings for an industrial fair that ultimately had to be cancelled after an earthquake struck in 1896. But the architect stayed on to help make good the damage, and was still here in 1903 to begin work on a memorial to the dead sheikh. The complex d'Aronco built incorporates a library and fountain as well as the tomb, and has just been completely restored.

The Şeyh Zafır complex is a hybrid of Art Nouveau and traditional Ottoman design. Purer examples of d'Aronco's work include the Casa Botter (p.107) on İstiklal Caddesi and the exquisite Tulip Fountain hidden in Laleli Çeşme Sokak in Galata.

Şeyh Zafır Mosque; Yıldız Caddesi, Beşiktaş; map D4

Take a souvenir snapshot alongside the brides at the
Ihlamur Pavilions

The souvenir photograph is as much a part of the modern Turkish wedding as it is of the British one, with one slight twist – the bride and groom often want to have themselves snapped against a suitably picturesque backdrop even if that means leaving their guests out of it. Couples who get married at the Beşiktaş Registry Office are particularly fortunate in that it is just across the road from one of the city's cutest but little-known monuments, the Ihlamur (Linden Tree) Pavilions, built for Sultan Abdülmecid in 1856 as a place to rest en route from Dolmabahçe Palace to the shipyards on the Golden Horn.

Over summer weekends visitors to the twin Ihlamur Pavilions are almost certain to find at least one happy couple draping themselves over the steps that provide access to the Ceremonial Pavilion (Mabeyn Köşkü) or posing beside the ornamental pool in front. The Entourage Pavilion (Maiyet Köşkü) has been converted into a café, so you can treat yourself to a tea while you wait to take your own pictures.

Ihlamur Pavilions (Ihlamur Kasrı); Ortabahçe Caddesi, Beşiktaş; Tue–Wed and Fri–Sun, summer 9am–5pm, winter 9am–3pm; small charge; map C4

Home in on the **novel gift ideas** to be found at the **Ortaköy Craft Market**

In Turkish Ortaköy means 'Middle Village', although it is unclear what it is meant to be in the middle of. No matter, because this is one of the coolest of Bosphorus suburbs, its past history as a Jewish and Christian settlement barely acknowledged by the crowds who flock in on Sundays to comb the crafts stalls set up in the network of narrow cobbled streets running down to the waterfront. It is the perfect place to browse for gifts to take home for friends who won't appreciate the standard tourist offerings. What's on offer varies with the month, but you can be fairly sure of finding one-off pieces of jewellery, hand-knitted hats, wooden toys and old Ottoman images reproduced on slithers of stone.

Why else would you head for Ortaköy? Well, the waterfront is dominated by a much-photographed mosque (p.118), which was designed by Nikoğos Balyan of Dolmabahçe Palace fame in 1854–5. However, most visitors tend to have their eyes more firmly set on the line-up of stalls selling baked potatoes with all sorts of different toppings. Alternatively, they come here for the trendy restaurants down by the waterside, including **Lavanta** (Mecidiye Köprü Sokak 16; tel: 212-227 2995), which is housed in a rambling wooden house, and **Banyan** (Salhane Sokak 3; tel: 212-259 9069), an award-winning restaurant dishing up a mix of dishes from Bali and Szechuan.

Ortaköy craft market; Sundays mid-morning to late afternoon; map G4

Delight in a **waterside view with a cocktail** on the terrace of the **Four Seasons at the Bosphorus**

When the sultans upped sticks and moved from the Topkapı Palace in Old Istanbul to the Dolmabahçe Palace in Beşiktaş in the mid-19th century most of the court moved with them. The result was the creation of a string of minor palaces along the European shore of the Bosphorus between Beşiktaş and Ortaköy, many of them now either lost or incorporated into the Galatasaray University campus.

In 2009 the 19th-century Atik Paşa Palace was restored and reopened as the luxurious Four Seasons at the Bosphorus Hotel. Boasting a 190m-long terrace, it has one of the city's most enviable locations, and few things could be more enjoyable on a summer's evening than to sit out here sipping a cocktail while eyeing up the action on the Bosphorus. Afterwards, enjoy a spectacular (and expensive) Italian meal at the hotel's poolside **Aqua Restaurant**.

Equally wonderful is the terrace of the **Çırağan Palace Kempinski Hotel** *(p.125)*, just a little further west along the Bosphorus. Or you could head on up to Ortaköy and have your cocktail in the maritime-themed, water-facing bar of the **Radisson Blu Bosphorus Hotel** (tel: 212-310 1500; map F4), a less architecturally magnificent but just as comfortable place to stay.

Four Seasons at the Bosphorus; Çırağan Caddesi 80; tel: 212-381 4000; www. fourseasons.com; map E3; see also p.178

Tuck into a delicious **İskender kebab** at the **Decorated Police Station**

The kebab is to Turkish cooking what fish and chips is to English cuisine, but just as true aficionados know that there is fish and chips and then there is fish and chips, so Istanbul showcases every kind of kebab, from the cheap-and-cheerful late-night döner to be snapped up for a couple of lira at the stands on the corner of Taksim Square to the perfectly cooked İskender kebab served in elegant surroundings at the Süslü Karakol (Decorated Police Station) in Beşiktaş.

The İskender kebab was supposedly the invention of a chef named İskender (Alexander) from 19th-century Bursa. He stuck his sword into the ground and used it to cook thin slithers of lamb without charring them, then layered the meat onto squidgy pide bread, added a dollop of fresh yoghurt, and dribbled tomato sauce and hot butter on everything. Done properly, it is one of the greatest of all the pleasures offered by Turkish cookery.

The Süslü Karakol was built in 1866 in a style that was frankly wasted on the police force. Today, however, it is one of the best places to sample an İskender kebab, as dished up by a company that claims descent from the original İskender. Too far to go? Then try one of the branches of **Konak** on İstiklal Caddesi which also serve up mouth-watering İskender kebabs – the one at 259 (tel: 212-244 4281) is the original and has the most eye-catching decor.

Kebapçı İskender; Süslü Karakol, Yıldız Yolu 6, Ihlamur, Beşiktaş; tel: 212-236 5571; daily L and D; map C4

Cheer on the 'Black Eagles' at **Dolmabahçe Stadium**, home to **Beşiktaş Football Club**

If you think the British have their football fanatics, then just wait until you see the Turks in action after a big match. This is a country where you'll be asked which team you support as often as you'll be asked where you come from. Cast your vote for any of the Istanbul big three – Galatasaray ('Cim Bom'), Fenerbahçe or Beşiktaş – and you will be pretty much guaranteed a friend for life.

Galatasaray, with a strip in red and yellow, play in Mecidiyeköy; Fenerbahçe, with a strip in blue and yellow, play over in Kadıköy; but Beşiktaş, with a strip in black and white, play right in the centre of things – their stadium is just a stone's throw away from the Dolmabahçe Palace. It is the only stadium in the world

where spectators can gaze out on Europe and Asia at the same time, and the great Brazilian footballer Pele once dubbed it the most beautiful pitch in the world.

Built in 1947, the stadium is named after İsmet İnönü, the second president of the Turkish Republic. There is a small museum for those who can't get enough of their heroes, and dotted about the nearby streets of Beşiktaş you will spot many statues of Black Eagles, paying homage to the team's local nickname.

Tickets to watch Beşiktaş and other football teams can be bought from Biletix (www.biletix.com).

Dolmabahçe Stadium (BJK İnönü Stadyumu); tel: 212-310 1000; www.bjk.com.tr; map B2

133

Golden Horn and Eyüp

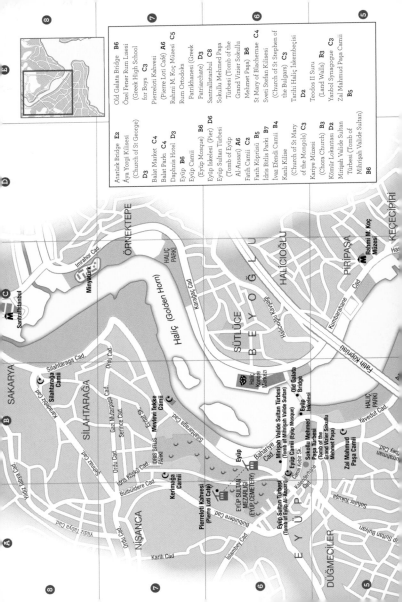

Golden Horn and Eyüp

0   100 200 300 400 500 m
0   100 200 300 400 500 yds

Admire the views of old and new Istanbul on a
ferry ride along the Golden Horn

Most visitors to Istanbul take a ferry ride from Eminönü, either to Kadıköy or Üsküdar on the Asian shore, or up the Bosphorus (p.156). Few realise that you can also take a boat trip up the Haliç, or Golden Horn, perhaps because the boats leave from an inconspicuous landing stage on the southwestern side of the Galata Bridge in front of the Storks nightclub. On a sunny day, this is a wonderful voyage – and it will set you back little more than the cost of a glass of tea.

Despite its romantic name, for much of the 20th century the Golden Horn was heavily industrialised, a legacy of the days when this was the main ship-building area. Recently, however, most of the industry has been relocated, and efforts are being made to rebeautify a part of the

city that was, in the early 18th century, renowned for its pleasure gardens. And where better to appreciate the end result than from the deck of a ferry?

You will get a chance to view several buildings that are either closed to the public, such as the restored 19th-century Bahriye Nezareti (Naval Headquarters) in Kasımpaşa, or better viewed from a distance, such as the Fener Greek High School for Boys, aka 'the Red Castle'. Of course, you can also admire the silhouettes of some of the city's great mosques, including the Süleymaniye and Yavuz Sultan Selim mosques.

Golden Horn ferry; for schedules see www.ido.com.tr; map pp.84–5, B2

Toss up the pros and cons of **cutting-edge artwork at SantralIstanbul**

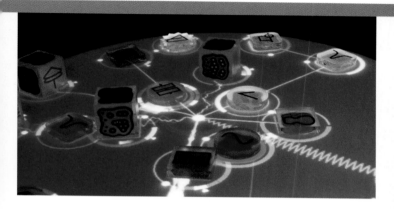

'But is it art?' The most enthralling place in Istanbul to ponder this conundrum has to be SantralIstanbul. This is Turkey's own take on the Tate Modern, housed inside what was the city's first electric power station, in service from 1911 to 1983.

The grounds of the power station, accessible by ferry to Sütlüce and then a 10-minute walk, or by a free minibus from Taksim, are now occupied by Bilgi University. The students here provide a regular audience for the conceptual and cutting-edge art exhibitions that take place right beside a Museum of Energy, which shows off the power station's original turbines and control room. Want to watch a robot sketching your portrait or a passport-photo machine playing fast and loose with your image? Then this is the place for you.

In keeping with the of-the-minute art installations, the campus plays host to two super-fashionable restaurants: a branch of **Otto** (tel: 212-427 1889) which has brought imaginative pizza creations to the city; and **Tamirane** (tel: 212-311 7309), an eatery that picks up on the rough edges of a traditional repair shop ('tamirhane' in Turkish) and renders them fashionably ironic.

SantralIstanbul; Birgi University Campus, Sütlüce; www.santralistanbul. org; Tue–Sun 9am–5pm; charge; map C8; free minibuses to Santral run hourly from in front of the Atatürk Cultural Centre in Taksim Square

Follow in the footsteps of a new sultan on the road to **Eyüp Mosque**, Istanbul's most holy site

The Eyüp Mosque, at the far end of the Golden Horn, was built over the grave of Ebu Eyüp el-Ensari, standard-bearer to the Prophet Mohammed, who died here when the Ummayyad Arabs laid unsuccessful siege to Constantinople in 668–9. His burial site was said to have been discovered after the Conquest of Istanbul in 1453, and ever after new sultans would travel here to be girded with the sword of Osman.

The new sultan would be conveyed to Eyüp by caique, landing close to where the tomb of the last sultan to be buried in Turkey, Mehmed V Reşat (1909–18), now stands. From there, he would process to the mosque along the Accession Road (Cülus Yolu), a route lined with beautiful burial complexes paid for by the rich and famous, including Hüsrev Paşa, the man who introduced the fez to Turkey from Tunisia, and Mihrişah Valide Sultan, the Genoese mother of Sultan Selim III.

The mosque is a very holy place, and the shrine is always packed with people praying. Ebu Eyüp el-Ensari is thought to have been fond of children, so many young boys are brought here to pray before their circumcisions. You will see them posing nervously for pictures with their families, dressed in crowns and costumes of satin and feathers.

Eyüp Mosque; tombs Tue–Sun until 4.30pm; take bus bus 44B or 99 from Eminönü or catch a ferry to Sütlüce and cross the Old Galata Bridge; map B6

ZAL MAHMUD PAŞA MOSQUE
While in Eyüp you might want to divert slightly along the coast road in search of the vast Zal Mahmud Paşa Mosque (map B5), a work of Sinan that could hardly look less like the cool, grey Süleymaniye. Zal was an unscrupulous individual who personally strangled Süleyman the Magnificent's son Mustafa but still went on to become grand vizier. He and his wife died on the same day in 1580 and are buried in this magnificent split-level complex.

Sip tea in memory of a French novelist at the famous
Pierre Loti Café

In 1876 the French novelist Pierre Loti (aka Julien Viaud) arrived in Istanbul and took up residence in Eyüp at the far end of the Golden Horn. There he engaged in a love affair with Aziyade, a Circassian beauty who was married to a wealthy merchant, their romance furnishing him with the material for his novel, also called *Aziyade*. Loti was almost equally enamoured with the Rabia Kadın Kahvesi, a café with a spectacular view over the Golden Horn and the two little islands at its western end. The original café no longer exists and the view from it is much changed since Loti's death in 1923, but the replacement is nonetheless very charming and on a summer's day few things could be more enjoyable than to grab a table outside and sip a tea or two in his memory.

The easiest way to get to the Pierre Loti Café is to take the cable car from the Eyüp waterfront. Afterwards, you can walk slowly back downhill again along a path that cuts through a cemetery full of Ottoman tombstones. Those decorated with a stone fez commemorate a man, those adorned with fruit and flowers are in honour of a woman.

Pierre Loti Café; Gümüşsyu Caddesi, Balmumcu Sokak 5, Eyüp; tel: 212-581 2696; daily B, L and D; map A6

Soak up the **atmosphere of long-lost Byzantium** at the Greek Patriarchate while exploring **Fener**

Most visitors to Istanbul spend the majority of their time in Sultanahmet with the odd side trip out to Beyoğlu. Few make it to Fener even though this was once one of the most important parts of the city, a stronghold inhabited by wealthy Greek-speaking descendants of the Byzantines. Known as Phanariotes, they often held high offices of state, but their mistake was to be too closely associated with the Greek push for independence in the 19th century, culminating in the execution in 1821 of the Patriarch, who had represented the Greek Orthodox community since Byzantine times, and the dispersal of much of the population to more far-flung corners of the city such as Büyükada.

GREEK PATRIARCHATE

Modern development has not been particularly kind to Fener, although the last decade has seen Unesco pump money into the area via the European Union to refurbish some of the old row-houses. Any exploration of Fener should start at the Patriarchate, where the Church of St George (*pictured*) can still claim to be the mother-church of Greek Orthodoxy worldwide. The current building only dates back to 1836, a time when many of the city's churches were rebuilt, but it does contain some fine fittings from older buildings on the site, including two rare mosaic icons. A casket contains the remains of St Euphemia, a local Christian supposedly thrown to a bear in c.305 for refusing an order to worship a pagan god.

FENER

Fener is built into the hillside, and presiding over it is the imposing building that housed the Greek High School for Boys on the site of a much older university. Built of red brick, it looks rather like an over-large Victorian water tower, albeit one with a spectacular view. To find it, look for a flight of steps that wends its way up Vodina Caddesi bypassing on the right the site of the erstwhile home of local historian Dimitri Camtemir (1673–1723) and then the small church of St Mary of the Mongols, enclosed inside a walled compound. Despite the poor quality of recent restoration of the latter, this is a very important church, the only one in the city to have preserved its shape intact from pre-Conquest days.

Another Church of St George closer to the water is also worthy of note, not so much for its architecture but because of a 13th-century prayerbook found there in 1906 – it turned out to have reused pages from 10th-century copies of works by the Greek

mathematician Archimedes of which no other versions exist.

Down by the waterside you will also see a couple of sturdy brick-built houses that suggest what Fener might have looked like in its heyday. Stranded in a sea of traffic, they also reveal how much the land level has risen over the years. One now contains a women's library, another a glass workshop.

Church of St George (Aya Yorgi Kilisesi), Greek Patriarchate; Dr Sadık Ahmet Caddesi; daily 9am–5pm; bus 44B or 99 from Eminönü; map D3

Stroll across the **old wooden Galata Bridge** from Eyüp to Sütlüce

Old postcards of Istanbul often feature the Old Galata Bridge, the wooden boardwalk erected in 1910. This had replaced a bridge constructed in 1875 along which passed a throng of people dressed in all the colours of the rainbow, as vividly described by the Italian traveller Edmondo di Amicis in his *Constantinople*, written in 1878.

In the age of the automobile the Old Galata Bridge no longer cut the mustard, and in 1994 it was replaced. The old bridge was then relocated further up the Golden Horn where its two sides jutted forlornly out from the shore, unable to meet and so serving no useful function. Happily, today they have been moved yet further west and reunited to provide a footbridge linking Eyüp to Sütlüce, now the last stop on the Golden Horn ferry ride from Eminönü. As you walk across it, be sure to look left to see the long and low pink Feshane (1833), where all the city's thousands of fezes were once manufactured.

Until recently, Sütlüce was a down-at-heel neighbourhood dominated by a vast abbatoir from 1923. This has been given a makeover to serve as the city's most architecturally distinguished conference centre, and the surrounding area is being renovated to provide a more appealing setting, with a waterside promenade now extending almost all the way up to the Bilgi University campus and SantralIstanbul art gallery (*p.139*).

Old Galata Bridge; take bus 44B or 99 from Eminönü to Eyüp; map B6

Dive below the waves in a **submarine** at the
Rahmi M. Koç Museum

Given the Golden Horn's history as an industrial centre throughout much of the 20th century, it is hardly surprising that when mega-businessman Rahmi M. Koç decided to create the country's first industrial heritage museum he picked the site of an old shipyard and anchor-making factory at Hasköy for its home. The Koç family are owners of premier white-goods firm Arçelik, so of course you will be able to find out more about the workings of a washing machine here as well as inspect a superb collection of vintage cars and other types of transport. Pride of place goes to a luxurious carriage from the train that conveyed Sultan Abdülaziz to Paris as the first Ottoman ruler to pay a peace-time visit to Europe in 1867.

Ottoman anchors turn out to have been manufactured in a building as beautiful as a mosque, but most people will probably spend more time across the road in the grounds of an old shipyard where several old shops, including an atmospheric pharmacy and toyshop, have been reconstructed. But this is also a very hands-on museum – visit over a summer weekend and you will be able to board a train for a short ride alongside the water to Sütlüce, sail upriver in a restored river tug or descend beneath the Golden Horn in a decommissioned submarine.

Rahmi M. Koç Museum; Hasköy Caddesi 5; tel: 212-369 6600; www.rmk-museum.org.tr; Tue–Fri 10am–5pm, Sat–Sun 10am–7pm; charge; bus 38T from Taksim or ferry to Hasköy; map C5

Shop for groceries in the traditional streets of Balat, Istanbul's old Jewish quarter

Midway along the southern shore of the Golden Horn, Balat, unlike its wealthy neighbour Fener, was a poor part of town with a large Jewish population. Today, there are still two functioning synagogues here although their congregations are much

diminished and they are difficult to visit without advance planning.

Recently, money has poured into Balat via Unesco and the EU in an effort to revive a struggling residential area right in the heart of the city, with a population mainly drawn from impoverished Eastern Turkey. Some of the largesse has gone to restore the attractive market area hiding away behind the worn-out relics of the old sea walls that once guarded against attack from the Golden Horn. This is a world away from the crowded, sometimes exasperating, Grand Bazaar. Here you can shop for fruit, vegetables and other household staples alongside a solidly local clientele. Don't try to barter here – you won't need to, as the hawk-eyed local matrons keep a keen eye out for the slightest sign of a price hike.

Along the edge of the market look for a gate in the wall that leads to the Yanbol Synagogue; its name commemorates the town in Bulgaria from which many locals once hailed. On the waterfront you will also see the Or-Ahayim Jewish Hospital, still hard at work today.

Balat market; Eski Kasaplar Sokak; daily; bus 44B or 99 from Eminönü; map C4

JEWISH MUSEUM
Over in Karaköy, near the entrance to the Tünel, the old Zülfaris Synagogue (Perçemli Sokak; Sun–Fri; charge) is now a museum devoted to the history of the Jews in Istanbul. The gallery has information about the wealthy Kamondo family who were bankers to the Ottoman court before the opening of the Ottoman Bank. Downstairs in the basement you can inspect Jewish wedding and circumcision scenes and household paraphernalia.

Run your finger over the rust inside the cast-iron
church of St Stephen of the Bulgars

Now here's a rarity – a cast-iron church designed by an Ottoman-Armenian architect that was cast in Vienna in 1871 and then shipped in pieces all the way down the Danube and across the Black Sea to be reconstructed on the shores of the Golden Horn at the point where Fener merges seamlessly into Balat. Replacing an earlier wooden church, St Stephen's was built to serve the Bulgarian Orthodox community, who were trying to shake off the control of the Greek Patriarchate up the road in Fener. Today, it is mainly used by Macedonians. The cast iron used to build the church weighed some 500 tonnes. However, this was thought to put less of a strain on the weak ground than concrete foundations would have done.

St Stephen's was designed in High Gothic style, which means that the interior is considerably more elaborate than the exterior might suggest. Over the years damp has caused some of the interior metalwork to rust; there's a striking contrast between the restored and unrestored sections.

In the 19th century there were plenty of other cast-iron churches, including some built by the British and sent to Australia, and others built by the French and sent to the Philippines and Peru. Today, however, St Stephen's is one of the last of its kind.

St Stephen of the Bulgars (Sveti Stefan Kilisesi); Abdülezel Paşa Caddesi/ Mürsel Paşa Caddesi; daily 9am–5pm; bus 44B or 99 from Eminönü; map C3

Discover the distinctive taste of **Black Sea cuisine** at the **Kömür Lokantası**

Over the last 20 years the population of Istanbul has exploded as people have poured in mainly from the troubled southeastern part of Turkey, but also from the Black Sea and central Anatolia. As a result, you can eat your way around the country without ever leaving the city.

A good place to start such a culinary tour would be the Kömür Lokantası in Küçükmustafapaşa (Cibali), a cheery restaurant that dishes up the distinctive – and often cabbage-flavoured – cuisine of the eastern end of the Black Sea to an appreciative local clientele. Don't come here expecting to admire the latest in fashionable tableware. Instead, this is somewhere to sample such delicacies as *lahana sarma* (stuffed cabbage leaves) and *lahana çorbası* (cabbage soup) as well as *hamsi tavası* (fried anchovies), a delicious winter treat.

Ready for more tasty local specialities? Then home in on **Hala** in Beyoğlu (İstiklal Caddesi 137/A; tel: 212-292 7004) to tuck into a bowl of *mantı*, tiny pasta packages wrapped round morsels of meat and doused in a garlicky yoghurt sauce that are a favourite of Kayseri in central Anatolia. For dessert, head for **Güllüoğlu** (Rıhtım Caddesi; tel: 212-293 0910) in Karaköy, which still makes the delicious pistachio-flavoured baklava that is virtually synonymous with Gaziantep in the southeast from a recipe dating back to the 1870s.

Kömür Lokantası; Müstantik Sokak 33, Küçükmustafapaşa; tel: 212-631 0192; daily B, L and D; bus 44B or 99 from Eminönü; map D2

Join the post-party diners for a revitalising bowl of *işkembe* soup overlooking the Golden Horn

Turkey is very much a soup-loving nation, with many residents getting the day off to a cracking start with a bowl of *mercimek çorbası* (lentil soup) supplemented with enough freshly baked bread to sink a proverbial battleship. Nor is that the only variety of soup to have earned its place in the nation's heart. Many *lokantas* (small local restaurants) can be relied on to rustle up a bowl of *domates çorbası* (tomato soup) garnished with cheese, a bowl of clear *tavuk çorbası* (chicken soup), or a bowl of *yayla çorbası* (highland meadow soup), a more idiosyncratic confection made from yoghurt, meat stock, mint and red pepper.

Most of these soups will find favour with visitors as well, but there is one variety that does take some getting used to and that is *işkembe çorbası* (tripe soup), a dish with a long-lived reputation as a hangover cure and therefore on sale in *lokantas* close to popular nightlife centres. In the past, the Golden Horn was well known for its many *meyhanes* (taverns) interspersed with *işkembecis* (restaurants selling *işkembe çorbası*), but although most of the taverns

are gone, the *işkembecis*, among them the picturesque **Tarihi Haliç İşkembecisi**, are hanging on in there. Indeed, there seem to be more of them with every passing year.

Spending the evening in Beyoğlu? Well, since 1960 the **Lale Işkembeci** (Tarlabaşı Bulvarı 3, Beyoğlu; tel: 212-252 696) has been helping out those who have overdosed on the *rakı*.

Tarihi Haliç İşkembecisi; Abdülezel Paşa Caddesi 315, Fener; tel: 212-534 9414; www.haliciskembecisi.com; daily B, L and D; bus 44B or 99 from Eminönü; map D2

The Rest of Istanbul

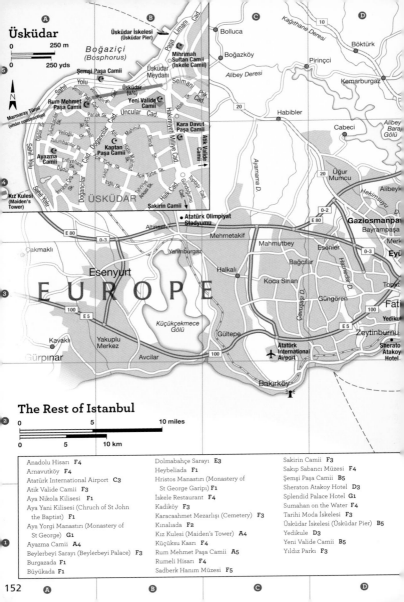

Üsküdar

0 — 250 m
0 — 250 yds

The Rest of Istanbul

0 — 5 — 10 miles
0 — 5 — 10 km

Enjoy the Princes' Islands without the summer crowds on **Burgaz and Kınalı islands**

Nestling to the north of the Sea of Marmara, the Princes' Islands are a group of nine islands, only five of them inhabited. Back in Byzantine times the islands were a dumping ground for deposed emperors and their families, who were often blinded to ensure they wouldn't return. Nowadays, however, the Princes' Islands act as a safety valve in summer, allowing wealthier residents to slip away at weekends to the calm of a traffic-free environment where horse-drawn phaetons still provide the only mode of public transport.

Most people head straight for Büyükada (Big Island), or at a pinch, for Heybeliada (Saddle-shaped Island), the second-largest island in the group. Want to escape the crowds? Then disembark from the ferry at Burgazada (Watchtower Island), which is dominated by the late 19th-century church of St John the Baptist. A short phaeton ride will take you to the contemporary Monastery of St George Garipi, built in glittering neo-Byzantine style. Alternatively, get off at Kınalıada (Hennaed Island), the smallest of the inhabited islands and the only one sans phaetons. The foreshore is dominated by a 20th-century mosque designed to evoke the shape of a boat, a rarity in a country where almost every new mosque would make poor Sinan weep.

Burgazada; map F1; Kınalıada; map F2

BOATS TO THE ISLES

Ferries leave Kabataş every 90 minutes or so (the first leaves at 6.50am), travelling via Kadıköy on the Asian shore, to the Princes' Islands. They stop at Kınalıada, Burgazada, Heybeliada and Büyükada, making it possible to island-hop your way through the day. There is also a fast ferry which leaves Kabataş every morning. Timetables are posted in the ferry stations; or you can check them at www.ido.com.tr. Be sure to confirm the time of the last ferry back.

Savour a *köfte* lunch with a panoramic view at St George's Monastery on **Büyükada**

Büyükada (Big Island) is the largest of the Princes' Islands in the Sea of Marmara and the most visited by tourists, who love to take a turn around the car-free streets in a horse-drawn phaeton. It also has the most to offer visitors, with fish restaurants running along the harbour, and a collection of hotels inland behind the clock tower.

If you take the 'big tour' of the island, you can hop out roughly halfway around the loop and climb up the steep, stone path that leads through pine forest to the Monastery of St George of the Bells. Like all the Princes' Islands, Büyükada was a monastic retreat, and St George's comes second in importance only to the monastery of Hagia Triada, better known as the Halki Seminary, on Heybeliada, where young men were trained as Greek Orthodox priests until 1971.

St George's dates back to the 10th century, although the present buildings are much more recent. According to legend, a 17th-century shepherd boy heard the sound of bells coming from underground and dug down to find an icon buried in 1204 as the renegade Fourth Crusaders descended on Constantinople.

The monastery grounds house a simple café where you can lunch on delicious fresh *köfte* (meatballs) and bread while gazing out over the azure sea at the whole of Istanbul. On St George's Day (23 April) every year pilgrims descend on the monastery in their thousands.

Aya Yorgi Kır Lokantası; Yüce Tepe Mevkii, Büyükada; tel 216-382 1333; daily 11am–11pm Apr–Nov, weekends only Dec–Mar; map G1

See the city from the water on a **cruise of the legendary Bosphorus**

If there is one feature of Istanbul that accounts for its extraordinary beauty, it must surely be the Bosphorus, the much-mythologised stretch of water that connects the Black Sea to the Mediterranean, giving it a strategic importance that has even caused wars. The Bosphorus takes its name from the Ancient Greek myth of Zeus and Io, a priestess with whom the god had an affair. In an attempt to protect Io from his vengeful wife Hera, Zeus had her turned into a cow. Hera responded by sending a gadfly to plague poor Io, who came eventually in her wanderings to this stretch of water, which now commemorates her in its name – 'cow passage'.

One of the highlights of any trip to Istanbul is a cruise along the Bosphorus. The best, at least for those with time available, are the twice-daily cruises provided by the İDO ferry company which operate from Eminönü. These travel right up to Rumeli Kavağı and Anadolu Kavağı, the twin settlements at the mouth of the Black Sea that do a roaring trade in quick fish lunches for the ferry passengers. Of the two, Anadolu Kavaği makes the better place to stop because you can climb up to the ruins of an old Genoese castle, offering panoramic views back down the Bosphorus.

The ferry journey is an adventure in itself, provided you show up early enough to bag a seat on deck. Topkapı Palace, Dolmabahçe Palace, Ortaköy Mosque, Rumeli Hisarı castle – you will see them all unfolding in front of you. No matter what the season, the views are always superb, although spring when the pinky-purple Judas trees come into bloom is especially pretty. The cruises also give you the best opportunity to admire the surviving wooden *yalıs* (waterfront mansions), all of them privately owned and so securely walled off from the roads that they can only really be viewed from the water. Throughout the journey, the crew come round selling tea, coffee and fresh orange juice. Once you pass Kanlıca, they also sell tubs of the yoghurt for which that suburb is particularly renowned.

EVENING CRUISES

If you don't have time for the İDO cruise, private companies also operating out of Eminönü offer shorter cruises as far as the first Bosphorus Bridge. In summer you can take to the water in the evening, a fantastic way to enjoy the scenery as the sun sets. There are also many party boats that offer evening cruises with food, music and dancing, as well as private launches that can be hired to organise your own entertainment; your best bet is to stroll along the promenade between Bebek and Rumeli Hisarı, and ask the captains of the many yachts moored there what they can offer. There are also themed cruises in summer, such as jazz evenings, that take to the water from Ortaköy. Look out for posters around town.

İDO Bosphorus cruises; www.ido.com.tr; tel: 212-444 4436; depart from Eminönü at 10.35am and 1.35pm year round; also a noon departure in summer; map E3

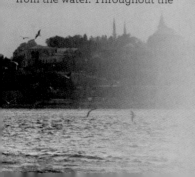

Learn about Turkish marriage and circumcision customs at the **Sadberk Hanım Museum**

torn down and replaced with modern apartment blocks.

The Sadberk Hanım Museum has two separate sections, one devoted to archaeology, the other to ethnography. It is in this second section that you will be able to learn about the three- and four-day marathons that used to mark the typical Turkish wedding. In particular, you will be able to study a reconstruction of a henna night, the local equivalent of a hen party but with much more elaborate customs, absolutely no alcohol and the bride-to-be retiring to bed with her hand bound up to allow a ball of henna to leave its mark on her palm and fingertips.

Here, too, you can find out about the traditions associated with circumcision, which usually takes place in Turkey when a boy reaches the age of eight or nine. To reward him for his ordeal the boy is allowed to play king for the day, reclining on a decorated bed while friends and relatives arrive with gifts to console him.

If you need a goal to encourage you to venture out along the Bosphorus shore, then how about a visit to the Sadberk Hanım Museum, one of Turkey's first privately owned museums? It is housed inside a fine old wooden *yalı*, one of the many waterside mansions that used to line both shores of the Bosphorus until the 20th-century mania for development saw most of them

Sadberk Hanım Museum; Piyasa Caddesi 25–9; tel: 212-277 2200; Thur–Tue 10am–5pm; charge; catch bus 25RE from Kabataş; map F5

Try *katmer* with soft goat's cheese in the stylish Muzedechanga at the Sakıp Sabancı Museum

Out along the European shore of the Bosphorus at Emirgan, the Sakıp Sabancı Museum is housed in what was once the stately home of one of the country's foremost industrialists. It is well known not just for the lovely views from its gardens, but also for the statue of a white horse copied from one of the Byzantine bronze horses in St Mark's Cathedral in Venice, stolen from Constantinople in 1204 by the Fourth Crusaders.

The Sakıp Sabancı Museum houses a fine collection of calligraphy as well as many lovely paintings by 19th- and 20th-century Turkish artists. It is also the venue for some of the city's best temporary exhibitions.

Also here is Muzedechanga, a wonderful restaurant serving Modern Turkish cuisine, which takes traditional ingredients and tweaks them for a more contemporary flavour. What to choose from the Peter Gordon-inspired menu? One dish certainly worth trying features *katmer*, a bread rather like an Indian paratha, served with a deliciously smooth goat's cheese and finely chopped green olives to add some bite. Eaten on the waterside terrace on a balmy summer evening, it is nothing short of divine.

Muzedechanga; Sakıp Sabancı Museum, Sakıp Sabancı Caddesi 22; tel: 212-323 0901; www.changa-istanbul. com; L and D; museum Tue–Sun 10am–6pm; charge; bus 25RE from Kabataş; map F4

Meander around the **backstreets of Arnavutköy**, one of the prettiest Bosphorus suburbs

If you take a cruise up the Bosphorus, you can hardly fail to notice Arnavutköy (Albanian Village), which acquired its rather unlikely name during the reign of Sultan Abdülmecit who resettled a group of Albanians here so that they could build pavements for his capitals. Today, Arnavutköy is an up-market suburb where the shore is lined with gorgeous wooden houses, many of them housing trendy restaurants and cafés.

It is well worth stopping off here to explore the backstreets, where an unusual number of fine wooden houses still survive. They were built in Art Nouveau style, but apparently using off-the-shelf components that could be added to a plainer wooden structure to give it the modern look. Right in the centre of the 'village' stands the imposing Taksiarchis Church, a Greek Orthodox structure from the 19th century which is a poignant reminder of more cosmopolitan times.

Down by the waterfront you might like to lunch at **Abracadabra** inside a wooden house painted the preferred rust-red colour known as Ottoman rose. Here the menu majors on regional delicacies and healthy eating. Instead of mezes, look out for what it calls tapas, including an unexpected duck *börek* (pastry).

Catch a ferry to Arnavutköy from Eminönü or bus 25RE from Kabataş; map F4
Abracadabra; Arnavutköy Caddesi 50/1; tel: 212-358 6087; daily B, L and D

Relish glorious **Bosphorus views** on a stroll along the promenade **from trendy Bebek to Rumeli Hisarı**

Over the last few years, the government has been working hard to lay promenades alongside long stretches of the Bosphorus, which has made the waterfront much more accessible than before. Few half-hour walks could be more pleasant than the one that starts at Bebek, with its pretty harbour and fashionable cafés, and ends in the shadow of Rumeli Hisarı, the huge castle constructed by Mehmed the Conqueror as he made plans to snatch Constantinople from the Byzantines.

As you amble along the promenade, you will be able to admire the yachts of the wealthy and watch the goings-on of the fishermen who haunt the shore from morning to night. This is a place to sample a helping of boiled corn-on-the-cob, a popular Turkish snack that is always on sale here, or to try your hand at blasting balloons floating out on the water, a popular Turkish (male) pastime.

Fancy a bite to eat before you start out? Well, **Happy Ever After** on Bebek's Cevdetpaşa Caddesi (24/A) does a fine line in cupcakes, while **Mangerie** (69) serves excellent breakfasts. You won't want to pass by **Rumeli Hisarı** without taking a turn round the interior (*below*). Then you can stop off at **Café Nar** (Yahya Kemal Caddesi 16/B) or **Sade Kahve** (Yahya Kemal Caddesi) for a sandwich.

To get to Bebek, catch a ferry from Eminönü or bus 25RE from Kabataş; map F4

RUMELİ FORTRESS

Composed of three main towers and a huge defensive wall that encircles a valley, the Rumeli Hisarı (Thur–Tue 9am–4.30pm; small charge) affords some terrific views. Although there is not much to see within the confines of the walls – a lonely minaret and a small amphitheatre sit in the centre among the foliage – the real fun of visiting the structure lies in clambering around the ramparts and climbing the steps to the dizzying heights of the towers, which stretch up to 28m high. Sufferers of vertigo beware!

Check out the lovely **Atik Valide Mosque**, finest of the many mosques in **Üsküdar**

Unlike exuberant Kadıköy, Üsküdar, just a little further north on the Asian Shore, has a reputation as a conservative neighbourhood, albeit one with a great deal to offer those who would like to visit some great Ottoman mosques that hardly see a foreign face from one year to the next.

As the ferry pulls into the terminal, you will spot immediately ahead of you the İskele (Harbour) Mosque, a work of Sinan dating from 1548 that would once have stood right on the shore so that the sultan could step straight from his caique onto the steps leading up to the ablutions fountain (said to have had one of the best views in the city). It was the first building in which Sinan tried out what went on to become his signature semi-domes.

If you follow the shoreline south towards the Maiden's Tower (p.165), you will soon come to the newly restored Şemsi Paşa

Mosque (1580), another work of Sinan, which sits in the lee of one of the radar towers built to guide shipping along the Bosphorus. From here, if you cut inland you will discover the considerably older Rum Mehmet Paşa Mosque, built in 1471 and looking remarkably like some of the city's Byzantine churches.

On the summit of the Toptaşı Caddesi hill, you will discover the huge Ayazma Mosque, the domed building that dominates the skyline as you land at Üsküdar. It dates back to 1760 and is decorated with miniature birdhouses. Returning to the area in front of the terminal and heading inland you can hardly miss the Yeni Valide Mosque, with what looks like an aviary attached to it but which actually turns out to house a tomb. Built in 1710 for Sultan Ahmed III's mother, this mosque has a delightfully peaceful courtyard in which to escape the traffic outside. But the star in the Üsküdar

mosque firmament has to be the Atik Valide Mosque, built high up on a hill as the centrepiece of an elaborate complex, complete with *medreses* (theological schools), a caravanserai, a *mekteb* (primary school) and an *imaret* (soup kitchen). Another work of Sinan, built in 1583, it was designed for Nurbanu Sultan, the wife of Sultan Selim II. You will probably find the delightful courtyard full of elderly men sipping tea in the midday sun.

ŞAKİRİN MOSQUE
Afterwards, for a complete change of pace, you could take a taxi over to the northeastern side of the sprawling Karacaahmet Cemetery to see the spanking-new Şakirin Mosque, which is that very rare thing in Turkey – a modern mosque with a touch of originality about it. Its interior was designed by Zeynep Fadıllıoğlu, best known for her work on the posh Ulus 29 restaurant. One look at the turquoise and gold mihrab (*pictured*) and all memory of Sinan will fly out of the window.

All the mosques are open daily but are best visited away from prayer times; ferries run to Üsküdar from Eminönü and Beşiktaş; map A5, B5, F3

Admire the **ornate interiors** of the Baroque **Beylerbeyi Palace**

If the queues to get into the Dolmabahçe Palace look daunting, forget it and hop on a ferry across to Üsküdar, then take a taxi or bus west to Beylerbeyi where you can visit the palace built there in 1865 by the Balyan family who were behind the Dolmabahçe. Although designed in the same Baroque style, Beylerbeyi Palace feels more restrained, if only because it is smaller. It was a particular hit with the Empress Eugenie, the wife of Emperor Napoleon III, who came here in 1869 on her way to the opening of the Suez Canal and may have embarked on an affair with Sultan Abdülaziz. Certainly, she had copies of the windows made to decorate the Tuileries in Paris.

The most beautiful room in the palace is adorned with a marble pool carved with dolphins so that the sight and sound of the running water would help residents keep cool in the high heat of summer. But a particularly conspicuous feature of most of the rooms is the delicate and detailed paintings of ships that decorate the ceilings and cornices. These were painted by the Polish artist Stanislas Chlebowski (1835–84),

whose greatest fan was Sultan Abdülaziz.

The palace grounds are lovely in summer, but it is also worth taking a stroll back into the adjoining suburb of Beylerbeyi where a cluster of cafés and fish restaurants, and a lovely fountain, gather together beside a mosque dating back to 1778.

Beylerbeyi Palace (Beylerbeyi Sarayı); Abdullah Ağa Caddesi, Beylerbeyi; Tue–Wed and Fri–Sun, summer 9.30am–5pm, winter 9.30am–4pm; charge; catch bus 15 from in front of the Üsküdar ferry terminal; map F3

Ferry-hop across to the romantic **Maiden's Tower**, launchpad for legends galore

Helen's may have been the face that launched a thousand ships, but the cute little Maiden's Tower, floating in the Bosphorus just off the shore of Üsküdar, has launched an equally enormous outpouring of paintings, photographs, postcards and posters. Sometimes known as Leander's Tower after a mix-up involving the tale of Leander who used to swim across the Hellespont every night to see his lover Hero, the Maiden's Tower is usually associated with the story of a princess whose father had been told that she would be killed by a snake bite. To guard against any such disaster, her father had her locked up in the tower where he could keep an eye on comings and goings. Unfortunately, a basket of figs was eventually delivered to the princess. Surprise, surprise – it turned out to contain a snake which jumped out and bit her.

Today, you can hop across to the tower, which was restored in 2000, from the waterside promenade. There is not a great deal to see once you have done so, although you can stop for a drink or even a full three-course meal (tel: 216-342 4747) here. The view back towards the city is predictably magnificent despite ongoing work on the Marmaray Project which involves digging a tunnel beneath the Bosphorus (due to end in 2011).

Maiden's Tower (Kız Kulesi); 9am–11pm; accessed by boat shuttle from Üsküdar; map A4

165

Pick out cheese and olives for a **picnic** in the narrow streets of **Kadıköy market**

Once the separate settlement of Chalcedon that was founded before Byzantium, Kadıköy, on the city's Asian shore, is an especially lively area with a large student population, guaranteeing it a vibrant nightlife and plenty of cheap and cheerful places to eat. Come here to get a feel for the real Istanbul, far from the famous attractions that attract the crowds.

If you head inland from the ferry terminal and then cut in to the right, you will come to market streets too narrow for cars to pass where you will find everything for sale aside from tacky souvenirs. It is a great place to scout out bargain footwear, old and new herbal remedies, a range of antiques and even a great choice of books about Turkey in English

at the **Greenhouse bookshop** (Dumlupınar Sokak 17).

The most colourful streets are those in the middle that are dominated by fruit-and-vegetable stalls, old-fashioned butcher's shops and fresh fish vendors. Everything here seems bigger, shinier and altogether more inviting than its supermarket equivalent – and if you stop off to eat at **Kadı Nimet Balıkçılık** (Serasker Caddesi 10/A; tel: 216-348 7389), an inviting small fish restaurant with a great local reputation, you can be sure that all the ingredients have been snapped up just minutes earlier from the stalls running round the outside.

Kadıköy market; ferries run to Kadıköy from Eminönü and Beşiktaş; map F3

Enjoy a **bar-hop along Kadıköy's Kadife Sokak** or an alcohol-free lunch at **Moda's old ferry terminal**

In Sultanahmet the most popular street for bar-hopping is Aybıyık Caddesi (White Moustache St), home to several of the city's hostels. Those in search of something more authentically Turkish head to Taksim and its lovely small *türkü* (folk music) bars. But for a stylish alternative, you can catch the ferry to Kadıköy, where Kadife Sokak boasts so many bars that it is commonly known as Barlar Sokak (Bar St).

What makes these bars so delightful is that they are housed inside restored Ottoman houses with *cumbas* (bay windows) jutting out into the street. What's more, most of them are themed to make them stand out. Fancy something nautical? Well, drop in on **Liman** (Harbour; 37), with lifebelts hanging on the walls ready to rescue those who've downed one too many. More interested in history? Well, **Isis** (26) tries its hand at a dose of Egyptology. More into an arty grunge scene? Then there's long-lived **Karga** (Crow; 16), which has a suitably darkened interior, the complete opposite of cheerful **Masal Evi** (Fairy-story House; 33), which is as colourful as a child's paintbox.

The Kadife Sokak bars are all small and cosy, and attract a regular clientele. The one snag is that the ferries stop running at 8pm. Fear not though, since there are *dolmuşes* (minibuses) to run you back to the European shore right through to midnight. They leave from near the ferry terminal.

Kadife Sokak, Kadıköy; map F3

MODA FERRY TERMINAL
Although 98 percent of Turks are Muslims, the heritage of a more cosmopolitan past means that not everyone holds hard to the Islamic prohibition on alcohol. If you want to save money, however, cutting out alcohol usually reduces bills dramatically. One great place for a 'dry' lunch is the beautifully restored old ferry terminal (Tarihi Moda İskelesi; Moda İskele Caddesi; tel: 216-449 926; map F3; *pictured*) at Moda, an up-market residential area attached to Kadıköy by antique tram.

Shake off the crowds at the petite **Küçüksu Pavilion**, a Dolmabahçe Palace in miniature

The smaller the 19th-century imperial palaces become the fewer visitors they seem to attract, which is great news for those who prefer to look around in peace and quiet. Smallest of all the palaces is the Küçüksu Pavilion, which sits beside the Küçüksu River where it flows into the Bosphorus between Anadolu Hisarı and Kandilli in an area that was once a popular pleasure ground known as 'the Sweet Waters of Asia'. It was built in Baroque style by Nikoğos Balyan in 1856–7 to serve Sultan Abdülmecit as a hunting lodge, and features a wonderful double staircase, an internal dome, beautiful parquet floors and the usual rash of Bohemian crystal, Hereke carpets and goldleaf galore.

Guided tours are compulsory and only available in Turkish, although since there are only eight rooms this is not much of a problem. Before you leave, walk round to the front of the pavilion which faces onto the Bosphorus. Since this is the side that would have greeted the sultan as he stepped off his caique, it is far more elaborate than the side that greets visitors today. Look out too for the gracious Mihrişah Sultan Fountain, erected in 1807 and regarded as the most elegant fountain along the Bosphorus.

Küçüksu Pavilion; Küçüksu Caddesi, Kandilli; Tue–Wed and Fri–Sun, summer 9.30am–5pm, winter 9.30am–4pm; small charge; bus 15 from Üsküdar ferry terminal; map F4

Romance your loved one over freshly landed **red mullet or sea bass** at the cute **İskele Restaurant**

Meyhanes (taverns) make great places for a lively night out over a fish supper, and Kumkapı *(p.42)* is fun for its atmosphere, but if you are after something more romantic, then nothing really beats the banks of the Bosphorus where fish restaurants jostle with one another to offer you a memorable dinner with the water lapping just inches away from your feet. A few favour flashy decor and live music. Most stick with a tried and tested recipe of crisp white tablecloths, attentive service and the freshest of ingredients.

At Rumeli Hisarı, in the shadow of Mehmet the Conqueror's brooding castle *(p.161)*, stands a pretty little ferry terminal, now decommissioned, which houses the popular İskele Restaurant, a fish emporium that likes to keep things simple. Probably the most popular dishes on the menu are *levrek* (sea bass) and *çıpura* (gilt-head bream), although here you can tuck into *istakoz* (lobster), *uzkumru* (mackerel), *lüfer* (bluefish) and *barbunya* (red mullet). *Kalkan* (turbot) is especially popular in spring, while winter sees *hamsi* (anchovies) take their place on the menu.

Back in neighbouring Bebek *(p.161)*, the fish restaurants with the biggest reputations are equally close to the water. **Poseidon** on Cevdetpaşa Caddesi (58; tel: 212-263 3823) runs a fine line in stuffed pumpkin flowers, while **Bebek Balıkçısı** (26/A; tel: 212-263 3447) is known for its *tuzda balık* (fish baked in salt).

İskele Restaurant; Yahya Kemal Caddesi 1, Rumeli Hisarı; tel: 212-263 2997; www.rumelihisariiskele.com; daily L and D; ferry from Eminönü to Bebek or bus 25RE from Kabataş; map F4

hotels

These days, the Istanbul hotel scene is as world-class as the monuments. No matter whether you want to stay in a small family-run hotel or a glitzy five-star with all mod cons, there will be something here to suit you, especially in Sultanahmet, the heart of tourist Istanbul and the best place to stay in terms of proximity to the main attractions. Having the Topkapı Palace only 10 minutes' walk from your shower is a big plus in summer when the heat can be exhausting. The only downside is the wearing attentions of would-be 'friends' who loiter with intent in Sultanahmet Square.

The second-best location – and best if a great choice of restaurants and a lively nightlife is most important to you – is Beyoğlu, where many of the four- and five-star hotels are within walking distance of Taksim Square. Although there are fewer hotels of character here, it is where you will find the historic and newly renovated Pera Palas Hotel.

Further afield, some of the city's finest and most expensive hotels line up along the Bosphorus with million-dollar views their calling card. For something a little more unusual, you could also stay on the Golden Horn at the Daphnis Hotel or in the Witt Istanbul Suites in fast-gentrifying Tophane.

HOTEL PRICES
Price for a standard room in high
season, including breakfast

€€€€ above €200
€€€ €120–200
€€ €75–120
€ below €75

Landmark Hotels

The Marmara Istanbul
🔲 Beyoğlu

Taksim Meydanı, Taksim; tel: 212-251 4696;
www.themarmarahotels.com; map p.101
F5; €€–€€€€

The lobby of this long-lived and
unmissable Taksim Square landmark
may be showing its age, but many
rooms have been renovated – be sure
to ask for one of the newer ones. The
views on all sides are jaw-dropping, with
an ace prospect of the square from the
rooftop gym (and vice versa, of course).

Çırağan Palace Kempinski
🔲 Beşiktaş

Çırağan Caddesi 32; tel: 212-326 4646;
www.kempinski.com; map p.121 E3; €€€€

A superb hotel in a restored Ottoman
palace on the European shore of the
Bosphorus, the Çırağan offers a range
of celebrity-attracting rooms and
suites, some in the original palace. The
glorious infinity pool is worth a visit
even if you are not staying (p.125). The
Ottoman and Italian restaurants are
renowned for fine dining.

Pera Palace Hotel
🔲 Beyoğlu

Meşrutiyet Caddesi 98/100, Tepebaşı;
tel: 212-251 4560; www.perapalace.com;
map p.100 C3; €€€–€€€€

Recently reopened after top-to-toe
renovation, this elegant 1892 hotel was
once home from home for travellers
on the Orient Express (p.94). Its guest
list reads like a roll-call of the great
and good of the 20th century, with a
sprinkling of spies and crime novelists
for good measure.

Money No Object

Ceylan Inter-Continental
🔲 **Beyoğlu**
Asker Ocağı Caddesi 1, Taksim; tel: 212-368 4444; www.ichotelsgroup.com; map p.101 F5; €€€–€€€€

This luxurious hotel within walking distance of Taksim Square commands superb vistas of the Bosphorus and city skylines. Turkish, French and Californian restaurants accompany bars, shops and a health and fitness centre complete with Turkish baths.

Swissôtel: The Bosphorus
🔲 **Dolmabahçe**
Bayıldım Caddesi 2, Maçka; tel: 212-326 1100; www.swissotel.com; map p.120 B3; €€–€€€€

An uphill walk behind the Dolmabahçe Palace, this massive hotel has a sprawling lobby with a slightly Japanese feel but fairly plain rooms gathered in two towers. The service is excellent, and there are superb views looking out over Topkapı Palace.

Conrad
🔲 **Beşiktaş**
Barbaros Bulvarı, Yıldız Caddesi; tel: 212-227 3000; www.conradhotels.com; map p.120 D4; €€€–€€€€

If it was good enough for Barack Obama, then it will surely be good enough for you too. The super-luxurious Conrad is a megalith of a hotel uphill from the Beşiktaş ferry terminal. The surrounds are nothing special, but once in your room you will have nothing to complain about – and the restaurants are of course excellent.

Hilton Istanbul
🔲 **Beyoğlu**
Cumhuriyet Caddesi, Harbiye; tel: 212-315 6000; www.hilton.com; map p.101 F5; €€–€€€€

Set in extensive grounds, this lavishly decorated 1950s hotel is still one of Istanbul's best. Recently fully renovated, it has 483 good-sized rooms and 15 suites, as well as seven bars and restaurants, a health club and spa, and – the ultimate Istanbul luxury – an outdoor pool. The one downside is a longish walk from Taksim Square.

Designer Chic

Ansen Suites
🟦 **Beyoğlu**
Meşrutiyet Caddesi 130, Tünel;
tel: 212-245 8808; www.ansensuites.com;
map p.100 C3; €€–€€€
This small all-suites hotel, just a hop
and a skip from the bustle of İstiklal
Caddesi, offers excellent value. Each
of the 10 sizeable suites is stylishly
decorated, with a fully equipped
mini-kitchen and large desk. The
French bistro on the ground floor
is fantastic.

Adamar Hotel
🟦 **Sultanahmet**
Yerebatan Caddesi 47; tel: 212-511 1936;
www.adamarhotel.com; map p.25 E3;
€€–€€€€
The recent beneficiary of a complete
makeover, the Adamar now boasts one
of the best city panoramas from its
rooftop restaurant. Rooms are spacious
and colourful. All the main attractions
of Sultanahmet and Beyazıt are within
walking distance, yet the Adamar still
feels slightly off the beaten track.

Empress Zöe
🟦 **Sultanahmet**
Akbıyık Caddesi, Adliye Sokak 10; tel: 212-
518 4360; www.emzoe.com; map p.25 F2;
€€–€€€€
A stone's throw from Topkapı Palace,
this cute hotel has 22 air-conditioned
rooms and suites, including budget
singles and doubles. The decor features
faux Byzantine wall-paintings, while
the ruins of a Turkish bath decorate the
garden. A spiral stairway makes access
to some rooms a bit tricky.

İbrahim Paşa
🟦 **Sultanahmet**
Terzihane Sokak 5, Adliye Yani; tel: 212-518
0394; www.ibrahimpasha.com; map p.25
E2; €€–€€€
This stylish hotel occupies a
renovated 19th-century Ottoman town
house beside the Hippodrome. The
19 rooms are on the small side (ask
for a new one for more space) and
simply furnished, but friendly staff
and excellent breakfasts compensate.
There's a spectacular view from the
roof terrace.

W Hotel
 Dolmabahçe

Süleyman Seba Caddesi 22; tel: 212-381 2121; www.wistanbul.com.tr; map p.120 C3; €€–€€€€

Istanbul's hippest hotel is housed in 19th-century row-houses built for the workers at the nearby Dolmabahçe Palace. What it lacks in views, it makes up for in its gorgeous Turkish-contemporary decor and über-chic glamour. Prices plummet off-season.

Witt Istanbul Suites
Tophane

Defterdar Yokuşu 26, Cihangir; tel: 212-393 79 00; www.wittistanbul.com; map p.84 D5; €€€

Located in the gradually gentrifying area of Cihangir, the Witt Istanbul Suites are chic and modern, with 17 suites decked out in cool brown, white and charcoal. Breakfast comes with organic ingredients where possible.

Hotel Kybele
Sultanahmet

Yerebatan Caddesi 35; tel: 212-511 7766/67; www.kybelehotel.com; map p.25 E3; €€–€€€

This colourful treasure house of Ottoman antiques and kilims in the centre of Sultanahmet is famous for a lobby decorated with hundreds of old lamps. Its 16 comfortable, air-conditioned rooms come with marble bathrooms, and there's a restaurant and a delightful courtyard.

Princes' Islands

Splendid Palace Hotel
Büyükada

Nisan Caddesi 23; tel: 216-382 6950; www.splendidhotel.net; map p.153 G1; €–€€€

This century-old wooden hotel looking straight onto the Sea of Marmara still clings to its colonial atmosphere, with columns holding up the high-ceilinged lobby and shutters on the windows. Bedrooms are fairly spartan; the best come with balconies.

Heart of the Action

Armada Hotel
◼ Sultanahmet
Ahırkapı Sokak 24; tel: 212-455 4455;
www.armadahotel.com.tr; map p.25 F1; €€
The unexpectedly large Armada Hotel
with identically decorated but cheerful
and distinctive rooms is in a quiet
Sultanahmet backstreet, a 10-minute
walk uphill to the centre of things. The
rooftop restaurant boasts superb views
of Hagia Sophia and the Blue Mosque,
while the lobby has an Ottoman-style
sitting area and a bar.

Sarı Konak
◼ Sultanahmet
Mimar Mehmed Ağa Caddesi 42–26;
tel: 212-638 6258; www.istanbul
hotelsarikonak.com; map p.25 F2;
€€–€€€€
A beautifully restored family-run
hotel in a Sultanahmet side street,
the Sarı Konak boasts a delightful
breakfast terrace with views of the
Sea of Marmara. Larger suites are
available in the building situated
right next door.

Richmond Hotel
◼ Beyoğlu
İstiklal Caddesi 445; tel: 212-252 5460;
www.richmondhotels.com.tr; map p.100
C3; €€€–€€€€
Located right on the hair-raisingly
busy pedestrian thoroughfare that
is İstiklal Caddesi in the heart of
Beyoğlu, the Richmond is a decent,
if unimaginative, modern hotel in
a recently renovated 19th-century
building. The Leb-i Derya Richmond
restaurant (p.113) and bar on the top
floor is perfect for a sunset cocktail.

Ottoman Imperial Hotel
▇ Sultanahmet

Caferiye Sokak 6/1; tel: 212-513 6151; www.
ottomanhotelimperial.com; map p.25 F3;
€€€–€€€€

Beside Hagia Sophia, this glamorous
new hotel could hardly be handier for
sightseeing. It is also hard to better
the view from its rear courtyard, which
overlooks the old Caferağa Medrese.
Traditionally decorated rooms and a
rooftop restaurant complete a great
all-round package.

Lush Hotel
▇ Beyoğlu

Sıraselviler Caddesi 12, Taksim; tel: 212-243
9595; www.lushhotel.com; map p.101 E4;
€€€–€€€€;

This turn-of-the-century apartment
building in the heart of Taksim has
been converted into a self-consciously
hip hotel, where 35 compact rooms are
decorated in styles from traditional
Anatolian through to trendy bunk beds
for adults. A sizeable buffet breakfast is
served in the basement restaurant.

Away from it All

Daphnis Hotel
▇ Fener

Sadrazam Ali Paşa Caddesi 26; tel: 212-531
4858; www.hoteldaphnis.com; map p.137
D3; €€–€€€

This small hotel was created out of
a row of Fener town houses across
the road from an old Greek school.
High-ceilinged rooms are wonderfully
atmospheric, and the restaurant at
the front overlooks the Golden Horn,
albeit across a busy main road.

Sumahan on the Water
▇ Cengelköy

Kuleli Caddesi 51; tel: 216-422 8000;
www.sumahan.com; map p.153 F4; €€€€

A cool 18-room hotel in a converted
rakı distillery on the Asian side of
the Bosphorus. Light-filled rooms are
individually decorated in contemporary
style with marble hamam-type
bathrooms. Many have great views over
the water. A private boat ferries guests
across to the European shore.

Rooms with a View

Four Seasons at the Bosphorus
▪ Beşiktaş

Çırağan Caddesi 28; tel: 212-381 4000; www.fourseasons.com; map p.121 E3; €€€€

Right beside the Bosphorus at Beşiktaş, this luxurious hotel consists of a renovated Ottoman waterside mansion with more modern wings on either side. To land the gorgeous Bosphorus views you need to opt for the pricier suites in the main building. Otherwise, in summer you can lounge on the lengthy terrace and enjoy them regardless.

Istanbul Holiday Apartments
▪ Beyoğlu

Galata Kulesi Sokak and Camekan Sokak; tel: 212-251 8530; www.istanbul holidayapartments.com; map p.100 C2; €€–€€€€

The uppermost of the fully equipped self-catering units in these two converted apartment blocks in trendy Galata come with to-die-for Bosphorus views. Size and decor vary considerably, but all are just steps away from delightful one-off shops and cafés.

Sheraton Ataköy
▪ Ataköy

Sahilyolu; tel: 212-560 8100; www.sheraton istanbulatakoy.com.tr; map p.152 D3; €€€–€€€€

The views from this high-rise hotel beside Ataköy Marina are so stunning that you won't immediately notice the decor that is also top-notch in every detail. The Cook Book restaurant dishes up great dinners downstairs. The one snag is that you're out on a limb here.

Historic Hotels

Ayasofya Konakları
■ Sultanahmet
Soğukçeşme Sokak; tel: 212-513 3660;
www.ayasofyapensions.com; map p.25 F3;
€€–€€€

Nine pastel-coloured wooden houses
lining a picturesque lane along the
Topkapı Palace's outer wall have
been converted into a delightful
guesthouse with fairly small rooms
decorated in a blend of contemporary
and Ottoman styles. The main
restaurant fills an old cistern (*p.33*).

Anemon Galata
■ Beyoğlu
Büyükhendek Caddesi 11; tel: 212-293
2343; www.anemonhotels.com; map p.100
C2; €€–€€€

A restored 19th-century town house
so close to the Galata Tower that
you can almost touch it, the Anemon
Galata is a rare Beyoğlu hotel that
sports Ottoman decor in its 21
rooms and 6 suites. The rooftop bar
and restaurant glory in fabulous
Bosphorus views.

Büyük Londra Oteli
■ Beyoğlu
Meşrutiyet Caddesi 117, Tepebaşı; tel: 212-
245 0670; map p.100 C4; €–€€

The original Ottoman furnishings
may look increasingly shabby
but this is the last of the Beyoğlu
hotels frequented by the likes of
Ernest Hemingway to have escaped
renovation. For some, the abundant
atmosphere and relatively cheap
prices will more than compensate for
any shortfalls on the decorative front.

The Four Seasons Sultanahmet
■ Sultanahmet
Tevkifhane Sokak 1; tel: 212-638 8200;
www.fourseasons.com/istanbul; map p.25
F2; €€€€

If you can afford it, this is the place
to stay in Sultanahmet. A converted
prison has become one of the city's
most luxurious and prestigious hotels.
Wonderful views of Hagia Sophia and
the Blue Mosque are complemented
by splendid decor, all mod cons, tip-top
service and excellent dining (*p.28*).

Yeşil Ev
■ Sultanahmet
Kabasakal Caddesi 5; tel: 212-517 6785;
www.istanbulyesilev.com; map p.25 F2;
€€€–€€€€

A beautifully reconstructed wooden
mansion in a picturesque alley right
in the heart of Sultanahmet. All 19
rooms are decorated Ottoman style,
and the garden restaurant has a great
reputation.

Essentials

A

Airports and arrival

Arrival by air

The national airline, THY (Türk Hava Yolları – Turkish Airlines; UK tel: 0844 800 6666; www.thy.com), flies to Istanbul from London Heathrow, Stansted and Manchester. Cheap direct flights are also offered by easyJet.

Most international airlines, including British Airways, have regular flights to Istanbul.

Airports

Istanbul's main airport is **Atatürk International Airport** (Atatürk Havalimanı; tel: 212 465 5555; www.ataturkairport.com) near Yeşilköy, 24km (15 miles) southwest of the city centre. A free shuttle bus links the international and domestic terminals.

Havaş (www.havas.com.tr) runs a bus service between the airport and city centre (half-hourly 6am–11pm). The journey time is about 45 minutes (often longer during rush hour). Taxis are faster and more convenient, taking only 20 to 30 minutes to the city centre, and costing around TL30. It is also possible to take the Metro to Zeytinburnu and change to the tram to reach the city centre.

Most low-cost airlines use **Sabiha Gokçen International airport** (tel: 216 585 5000; www.sgairport.com) at Pendik on the Asian side of Istanbul.

Hourly Havaş buses connect it with Taksim Square.

Arrival by rail

Allow approximately three days for the journey from London to Istanbul. The InterRail Global pass allows various periods of unlimited travel in 30 European countries, including Turkey (for details tel: 08448 484 064; www.raileurope.co.uk).

The city's two main stations are **Sirkeci** (Europe; tel: 212 527 0050), and **Haydarpaşa** (Asia; tel: 216 348 8020).

C

Climate

Istanbul has a temperate climate, with cool, wet winters and warm, dry summers. The best times to visit are from April to June, and from September to October.

Clothing

Locals dress modestly, and avoid shorts and skimpy tops even in high summer. When visiting mosques, wear long trousers or a skirt reaching below the knee, with a long-sleeved shirt or blouse; women should cover their heads. At the Blue Mosque, scantily clad tourists are given robes to wear while visiting. Remember to remove your shoes before entering a mosque or a Turkish home. Evenings can turn cool, especially in spring and autumn, so it is worth packing an extra layer or two.

Customs

There is no limit on the amount of foreign currency that may be brought into the country, but no more than US$5,000 worth of Turkish lira can be imported or exported. You can bring the following when you leave Turkey: 200 cigarettes, 10 cigars, two bottles of wine, 1kg of coffee and 0.5kg of tea. Check www.gumruk.gov.tr for full details.

Buying and exporting antiquities is strictly forbidden in Turkey. If you buy an antique, make sure that it is from a reputable dealer, who can provide an invoice *(fatura)* stating its value and organise an export permit.

D

Disabled travellers

Few major sights have elevators or ramps, and wheelchairs are not permitted inside mosques. However, green buses do admit wheelchairs, and most tram stations are accessible. Voice recordings announce each tram stop. Disabled public toilets are a rarity.

E

Electricity

Turkey uses a 220-volt, 50-cycle current. You will need an adaptor for continental-style two-pin sockets; American 110-volt appliances will also require a transformer.

Embassies and consulates

Most countries have consulates in Istanbul, although the embassies are in Ankara:

Australian Consulate, Asker Ocağı Caddesi 15, Elmadağ; tel: 212 243 1333
British Consulate, Meşrutiyet Caddesi 34, Tepebaşı, Beyoğlu; tel: 212 334 6400
Canadian Consulate, İstiklal Caddesi 373/5, Beyoğlu; tel: 212 251 9838
Irish Honorary Consulate, Acısu Sokak 5/4, Maçka; tel: 212 259 6979
US Consulate, Kaplıcalar Mevkii 2, Istinye; tel: 212 335 9000

Emergencies

In an emergency your best bet is to ask your hotel for help; otherwise, call

155 for police
110 for the fire brigade
112 for an ambulance

F

Festivals

April: Istanbul International Film Festival
May: Festival of Gypsy Music, International Theatre Festival and Anniversary of the Turkish conquest of Istanbul in 1453 (29 May)
July: International Jazz Festival
September: Istanbul Biennial
October: Efes Pilsen Blues Festival, Akbank Jazz Festival and Istanbul Marathon

G
Gay and lesbian travellers
Although Istanbul has a lively gay
scene, the city still has a long way to
go to achieve the levels of liberalism
in cities such as London, New York
and Paris. Public shows of affection
are unwise.

H
Health
The main health hazards are the sun
and the risk of diarrhoea, so use sun
block and a hat during the summer
and be careful with food and drinks.

Healthcare and insurance
There is no free healthcare for
visitors to Turkey. You should
have an adequate insurance policy,
preferably including cover for an
emergency flight home. However,
if you don't have insurance, few
Turkish hospitals are prohibitively
expensive. Private hospitals offer
excellent treatment.

Vaccinations
There are no compulsory
immunisation requirements for
Turkey. Up-to-date vaccinations for
tetanus, polio, typhoid and hepatitis A
are recommended.

Hospitals and pharmacies
The American Hospital (Amerikan
Hastanesı) in Nişantaşı (Guzelbahce
Sokak 20; tel: 212 444 3777) is good,

clean and efficient with English-
speaking staff.

Aykut Eczanesi (Sıraselviler
Caddesi 135; tel: 212 243 1785) is
a 24-hour pharmacy in Taksim.
There's also a good English-speaking
pharmacy in Sultanahmet (Divan
Yolu Caddesi 60; tel 212 513 5035).
Pharmacies generally rotate the night
shift; notices in the window give
details of the current 'nöbetci'.

Hours and holidays
Opening hours
Banks are generally open Mon–Fri
8.30am–noon and 1.30–5pm, while
currency-exchange offices open daily
8am–8pm. The main post offices run
Mon–Sat 9am–5pm.

Shops usually open Mon–Sat
9.30am–7pm. Many tourist shops stay
open later and on Sundays, as do malls
and most stores on İstiklal Caddesi.

Museums generally open Tues–Sun
9.30am–5pm.

Mosques are open to tourists
except during prayer times, especially
on Fridays, the Muslim holy day.

Secular holidays
Banks, post offices, government
offices and other businesses will be
closed on the following:
1 Jan: Yılbaşı – New Year's Day
23 Apr: Ulusal Egemenlik ve Çocuk
Bayramı – National Sovereignty and
Children's Day
19 May: Gençlik ve Spor Günü –
Youth and Sports Day
30 Aug: Zafer Bayramı – Victory Day

29 Oct: Cumhuriyet Bayramı – Republic Day

Religious holidays
The two national religious holidays (Şeker Bayramı and Kurban Bayramı) are marked by three and four days off respectively. The dates vary each year according to the Islamic calendar.

L
Language
Around Sultanahmet and the main tourist sights, many people will be able to speak English. Locals usually welcome any attempt to speak their language.

M
Maps
To get hold of any additional maps of Istanbul, ask at the tourist office in Sultanahmet Park. Another good source for maps is the Istanbul Kitapçısı (379 İstiklal Caddesi, Beyoğlu; tel: 212 292 7692; www.istanbulkitapcisi.com), which also stocks a range of books about Istanbul in English.

Media
Television
State-owned TRT (Türkiye Radyo ve Televizyon) broadcasts several nationwide channels. Many hotels have satellite television with BBC World, CNN and Sky, plus German, French and other European channels.

Radio
You can pick up the BBC World Service and Voice of America on short-wave radio. There are regular news summaries in English on TRT-3 (88.4, 94.0 and 99.0 MHZ).

Newspapers
There are two English-language dailies: *Today's/Sunday's Zaman* and *Hurriyet Turkish Daily News*. You can buy British newspapers in Sultanahmet and Taksim. *Time Out Istanbul* is a monthly listings magazine in English.

Money
Currency
Turkey uses the Türk Lira (TL). At the time of writing, £1 was equivalent to TL2.30 and $1 to TL1.7. Coins come in 5, 10 and 25 *kuruş* and 1TL denominations. Notes come in 5, 10, 20, 50, 100 and 200 TL units.

Banks and currency exchanges
The most efficient banks are Yapı Kredi, Garanti Bankası, HSBC and Akbank. Shop around for the best rates, which are always better in Turkey than in the UK. You can also change money at post offices.

Cash machines
The fastest and easiest way to get cash is to use an ATM; these are commonplace throughout the city.

Credit cards
Credit and debit cards (but not American Express) are widely

accepted in hotels, restaurants,
tourist shops and car-hire companies.
Some shops may ask you to pay
extra to cover the card company's
commission.

Tipping
It is customary to leave 10–15 percent
at restaurants, and to round taxi fares
to the nearest lira. Hamam staff also
appreciate a 10 percent tip.

Taxes
VAT (KDV) is charged at 8 to 25
percent depending on the item.
Foreigners are entitled to a refund;
for advice on how to reclaim KDV on
pricy items consult the shop staff.

P
Police
Turkey's police officers wear
distinctive blue uniforms and there
is a police station (karakol) in every
neighbourhood. The Trafik Polisi look
after road accidents, badly parked
vehicles, etc. To call the police in an
emergency dial 155.

The Istanbul tourist police are
based at Yerebatan Caddesi 6,
Sultanahmet; tel: 212 527 4503.

Post
Istanbul's main post office is in
Büyük Postane Caddesi (turn left,
facing the ferries, at the Sirkeci tram
stop; p.95); other branches are in the
Grand Bazaar and at Galatasaray
Square.

Stamps can also be bought at
shops selling postcards. Post boxes
are scarce, so try posting your mail
from your hotel desk or at the post
office (PTT). There are usually
three slots, marked şehiriçi for local
addresses, yurtiçi for destinations
within Turkey and yurtdışı for
international mail.

It costs 1.40TL to send a 50g letter
to the UK or US from Turkey, while a
postcard is 0.80TL.

R
Religion
Ninety-eight percent of Turks are
Muslims. Istanbul also has tiny
Christian and Jewish populations
with their own churches and
synagogues. Details of religious
services can be obtained from the
tourist office.

S
Smoking
A full ban on smoking in all enclosed
spaces, including bars, restaurants and
cafés, came into effect in mid-2009.

T
Telephones
The dialling code for Turkey is +90.
For intercity calls (including calls to
the Asian side of the Bosphorus), dial
0, then the area code (212 in European
Istanbul; 216 on the Asian side), then
the number. To make an international

call, dial 00 then the country code (1 for the US, 44 for the UK), followed by the area code (without the initial 0) and number.

You can make domestic and international phone calls from PTT offices, or phone boxes on the street. These accept either credit cards or telephone cards *(telekart)*, which can be bought at PTT offices and at some newsstands and kiosks.

Mobile phones

Turkey is on the GSM mobile network. Buying a pay-as-you-go SIM card is a straightforward procedure, with cards available from Türkcell, Avea or Vodafone. Türkcell has a stand at Atatürk Airport; buy a SIM card there and it will be activated before you even reach your hotel.

Time Zones

Turkish time is GMT plus two hours in winter and plus three hours in summer.

Toilets

Public toilets *(tuvalet)* are becoming smarter and more common; you usually pay at least 75 *kuruş*.

Toilets are occasionally of the hole-in-the-floor variety, and often lack paper, so it is a good idea to carry some with you. Never put paper down the lavatory; it should go in the receptacle provided. Ladies' toilets are marked *kadın* or *bayan*, gentlemen's *erkek* or *bay*.

Tourist information

Istanbul's main tourist office is in Sultanahmet, near the tram stop (tel: 212 518 8754).

Turkish tourist offices abroad

UK: 4th Floor, 29–30 St James's Street, London SW1A 1HB; tel: 020 7839 7778; www.goturkey.co.uk

US: 821 UN Plaza, New York NY 10017; tel: 212 687 2194; www.tourismturkey.org

Tours and guides

Official English-speaking guides can be hired through travel agencies and the better hotels. They are usually friendly and knowledgeable, and can prove invaluable if your time is limited. Freelance guides also hang around at the entrance to Topkapı Palace and the Aya Sofya, but don't let yourself be pressured into hiring one, make sure you agree on a price before you set out and watch out for street touts.

Transport
Abkil

A small stainless-steel button on a plastic holder with a computer chip inside, this is an electronic transit pass, available from kiosks in Eminönü, Taksim Square and other main transport interchanges. It is a hassle-free means of paying for travel on buses, trams, the Tünel, Metro and ferries. Simply press the Abkil against the little circular socket at the turnstile (or at the front of a bus), and the fare will be deducted electronically. When most of its value is used up, recharge it at an Abkil kiosk.

Buses
Istanbul city buses are cheap and frequent, but can be crowded, particularly during rush hours. Buy a flat-rate ticket from a kiosk before boarding.

Dolmuş
Nowadays a *dolmuş* is usually a minibus that shuttles back and forth along a set route for a fixed fare. The departure and destination are indicated in the windscreen. *Dolmuş* stops are marked by a sign with a 'D'.

Ferries
For ferries, buy a jeton before departure from the ticket desk (*gişe*), where prices and timetables are displayed; otherwise, use your Abkil. Ferry timetables change from winter to summer; check www.ido.com.tr.

The main departure point for Istanbul's ferries is Eminönü, between Sirkeci Station and Galata Bridge. The jetty nearest the bridge is for trips along the Bosphorus; next are the Üsküdar and Kadıköy jetties for boats to the Asian shore; finally comes the car ferry to Harem, near Haydarpaşa Railway Station, also on the Asian side.

Ferries along the Golden Horn also depart from Eminönü on the far side of the Galata Bridge.

Another major ferry terminal is Kabataş, further up the Bosphorus on the European shore. Ferries leave here for the Princes' Islands and the Asian shore.

Seabus catamaran
Sleek, modern catamarans zoom around the city at rush hour, and out to the Princes' Islands from Kabataş several times daily in summer. There are even catamarans to Yalova and Bandırma on the Sea of Marmara's southern shore for access to Bursa and İzmir.

Taxis
Istanbul's bright yellow taxis are mostly powered by clean-burning natural gas. They can be hailed in the street, picked up at a rank or ordered by telephone from your hotel. All taxis have meters and are required by law to run them. Most drivers are honest, but a few may try to rip you off by 'adjusting' the meter or doing conjuring tricks with your money. Few drivers speak English, so it is worth writing your destination on a piece of paper.

Trains
The suburban rail service from Sirkeci to Yeşilköy near Atatürk International Airport transits Kumkapı and Yedikule. Buy a flat-rate ticket on the platform or use your Akbil. The Marmaray Tunnel (operational by around 2012) will link Sirkeci Station with a new station at Üsküdar via a submerged tunnel.

Trams

Istanbul has a very useful tram service *(tramvay)* which runs from Aksaray to Sultanahmet, through Sirkeci/Eminönü, across the Galata Bridge and as far as Kabataş (Dolmabahçe Palace). The tram is also useful for getting to the airport, if you change to the Metro at Yusufpaşa or Zeytinburnu. Trams run every 5 minutes or so during peak hours.

For a map of the tram, metro and rail system, see www.istanbululasim.com.tr.

A restored 19th-century tram *(p.106)* runs along İstiklal Caddesi from the Tünel to Taksim Square.

Metro

The Metro runs from Aksaray to Istanbul's mammoth Topkapı *otogar* (intercity bus station) at Esenler, where you can board a bus to anywhere in Turkey.

Funiculars

Istanbul's tiny underground train, the Tünel *(p.103)*, climbs the steep hill from Galata Bridge up to Pera every few minutes taking 90 seconds to reach the top. A second funicular links Kabataş ferry and tram terminal with Taksim Square.

V

Visas and passports

UK, US and Irish citizens need a full passport and a 90-day visa that can be purchased from the visa desk before going through passport control on arrival in Turkey. The cost is £10, US$20 or €10 in cash.

W

Websites

Useful websites include:
www.pukkaliving.com – A hip guide to the city that has particularly good ideas for shopping and nightlife.
www.istanbul.com – Useful and well laid out, this site is supported by the tourist board and features plenty of ideas and city information.
www.iksv.org – Istanbul Foundation for Culture and Arts site, with information about classical, art, jazz and film festivals.
www.biletix.com – Ticketmaster's Turkish branch; a great source for concert information and buying tickets online.

Women travellers

Istanbul is generally a very safe place for women, although harassment in tourist areas can be irritating. Women accompanied by a man are less likely to attract unwanted attention. The best strategy is to dress modestly, with long trousers or a long skirt, and a long-sleeved, loose-fitting top. Walk purposefully and avoid making eye contact. People will generally accept a firm 'no'. If not, raise your voice and a dozen knights in shining armour will rush to your aid.

Index

Index

Insight Select Guide: Istanbul
Written by: Pat Yale
Edited by: Alexander Knights
Layout by: Ian Spick
Maps: James Macdonald
Picture Manager: Steven Lawrence
Series Editor: Cathy Muscat
Photography: All pictures by APA/Rebecca Erol
except: Istockphoto 7T, 7B, 9T, 30, 37, 59, 65, 87, 110,
158, 164; Pascal Meunier 17B; Leonardo 17T, 105;
Axiom 18, 22, 91, 97; 4 Corners 26-27; Ardiles Acre 28;
Turkish Culture and Tourism 33, 51, 118; Tcp909 95;
Courtesy Alaturka Cooking School 36; Getty Images
50, 60-61, 116; Fotolia 64; Bombardier 70-71; Corbis 72;
Josep Renalais 73; Courtesy Aristane Restaurant 74;
Courtesy Zeyrekhane Restaurant 80; Ed Clayton 112;
Kavakklidere 115; Courtesy KV Café 117; Cacak Os-
man Tandik 122; Zuma 123; Kempinski 125; Rebecca
Erol 127; Chapultec 129; Four Seasons 131; AWL Im-
ages 134; Pictures Colour Library 138; Alara Orhon
139; Anastassiya 140; Mary Evans 144; Rahmi M.
Koc Museum 145; Murzedechaga 159; Donny Hoca
162-163; WOW.turkey.com 167; Frank Kovalchek 168;
Hotel Ibrahim Pasha 174; Kmail Yilmaz 175; Admar
Hotel 176T; Richmond Hotels 177; Ciragan Palace
178; Peter Vitale 179T

Acknowledgements: Pat Yale would like to thank
Angela Moore at the Four Seasons Sultanahmet for
generously sharing her knowledge of all things edible
and drinkable, and the staff at Siirt Şeref restaurant
who introduced her to the pleasures of the buryan
kebab. Thanks, too, to Eveline Zoutendijk for trying to
teach her to cook like a Turk. Rene Ames reminded
her of several city quirks, while Rebecca Erol drew
her attention to the hidden delights of the Crimean
Memorial Church. Saffet Emre Tonguç kindly shared
his life-long knowledge of the city, while Jennifer
Gaudet, Mehmet Girgıç and Veliye Marti spared time
to discuss ancient handicrafts with her. Finally, Julie
Dowdall and Kate Drummond were always there to
share in the research.

First Edition 2010
© 2010 Apa Publications GmbH & Co.
Verlag KG Singapore Branch, Singapore.
Printed by CTPS-China

Contacting the Editors
We would appreciate it if readers would alert us to
outdated information by writing to:
Apa Publications, PO Box 7910, London SE1 1WE,
UK; email: insight@apaguide.co.uk

Distribution
Distributed in the UK and Ireland by:
GeoCenter International Ltd
Meridian House, Churchill Way West, Basingstoke,
Hampshire RG21 6YR; tel: (44 1256) 817 987; email:
sales@geocenter.co.uk

Distributed in the United States by:
Langenscheidt Publishers, Inc.
36-36 33rd Street 4th Floor, Long Island City, New
York 11106; tel: (1 718) 784 0055; email: orders@
langenscheidt.com

Distributed in Australia by:
Universal Publishers
1 Waterloo Road, Macquarie Park, NSW 2113;
email: sales@universalpublishers.com.au

Distributed in New Zealand by:
Hema Maps New Zealand Ltd (HNZ)
Unit 2, 10 Cryers Road, East Tamaki, Auckland
2013; email: sales.hema@clear.net.nz

Worldwide distribution by:
Apa Publications GmbH & Co. Verlag KG
Singapore, 7030 Ang Mo Kio Ave 5, 08-65 North-
star @ AMK, Singapore 569880; tel: (65) 6570 1051;
email: apasin@singnet.com.sg

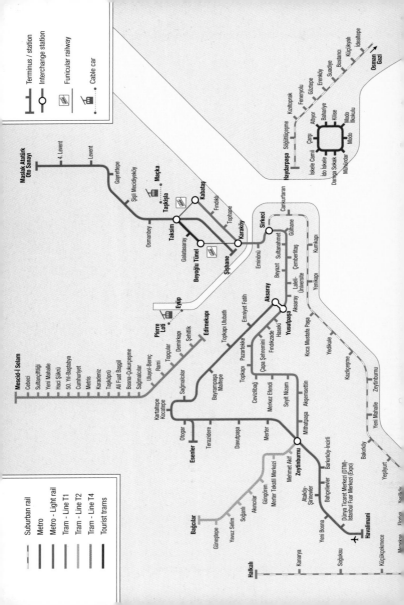